Leckie
the education publisher
for Scotland

National 5
HISTORY

For SQA 2019 and beyond

D1363097

Revision + Practice
2 Books in 1

Published by
Leckie
An imprint of HarperCollinsPublishers
Westerhill Road, Bishopbriggs, Glasgow, G64 2QT
T: 0844 576 8126   F: 0844 576 8131

leckiescotland@harpercollins.co.uk   www.leckiescotland.co.uk

HarperCollinsPublishers, 1st Floor, Watermarque Building, Ringsend Road, Dublin 4, Ireland

Publisher: Sarah Mitchell
Project Managers: Harley Griffiths and Lauren Murray

Special thanks to
QBS (layout and illustration)

Printed and bound in the UK using 100%
Renewable Electricity at CPI Group (UK) Ltd

A CIP Catalogue record for this book is available from the British Library.

Acknowledgements
We would like to thank the following for permission to reproduce photographs. Page numbers are followed, where necessary, by t (top), b (bottom), m (middle), l (left) or r (right). P10t Jupiterimages, P10b SuperStock, P13 Popperfoto / Getty Images, P17 © Scottish Life Archive, National Museums of Scotland. Licensor www.scran.ac.uk, P19 Reproduced with the permission of Strathclyde Partnership for Transport, P20 © Scottish Life Archive, National Museums of Scotland. Licensor www.scran.ac.uk, P21 © Hulton-Deutsch / CORBIS, P22 Alphonse Leong / Shutterstock.com, P23 © The Art Archive / Superstock, P25m Getty Images, P26 Popperfoto / Getty Images, P30 SSPL via Getty Images, P31 © Imperial War Museums (Q 20002), P33 © Scottish Life Archive, National Museums of Scotland. Licensor www.scran.ac.uk, P35 Millicent Fawcett – Getty Images, P35 Emmeline Pankhurst – Getty Images, P35 John Maclean – Getty Images, P38 British Library / Robana via Getty Images, P43 English School, P51 National Records of Scotland, BR-FOR-4-34-223, P52 Lairich Rig, P54b Getty Images, P58 Getty Images, P60 © Scottish Life Archive, National Museums of Scotland. Licensor www.scran. ac.uk, P62 By Permission of People's History Museum, P64 Time & Life Pictures, P65t Getty Images, P65b Getty Images, P67 Alinari via Getty Images, P69 Getty Images, P70 Getty Images, P75t Popperfoto / Getty Images, P75b Bundesarchiv, Bild 183-R15068 / CC-BY-SA, P82 Getty Images, P83 Getty Images, P85b Time & Life Pictures / Getty Images, P86 NY Daily News via Getty Images, P89 Getty Images, P92 Getty Images, P95t Getty Images, P98 Time & Life Pictures/ Getty Images, P103 Gamma-Rapho via Getty Images, P104 Getty Images, P105 Nikita Khrushchev – Getty Images.

Paper A, Section 1, Part 1, Source B:
About the crowning of Robert Bruce as King in 1306.
Adapted from A.D.M. Barrell, *Medieval Scotland*, 2000, Cambridge University Press

Paper A, Section 1, Part 5, Source A:
Describes the use of tanks during the Battle of Cambrai 1917.
Adapted from *Britain at War 1914–1919*, Craig Mair, John Murray

Paper A, Section 1, Part 5, Source B:
Adapted from *Voices of the First World War* by Max Arthur

Paper A, Section 2, Part 1, Source A:
Written by Gerald of Wales about King Henry II.
Reprinted by permission of HarperCollins Publishers Ltd © 2012 Daniel Jones

Paper A, Section 2, Part 1, Source A:
Adapted from *An Illustrated History of the Crusades* by W.B Bartlett, The History Press

Paper A, Section 3, Part 1, Source C:
Describes Richard I towards the end of the Third Crusade.
Adapted from *The Crusades*, Terry Jones and Alan Ereira, BBC Books.
Reproduced by permission of Random House

Paper A, Section 3, Part 4, Source A:
The impact of the Great Depression on German politics.
Adapted from Spartacus Educational website:
http://www.spartacus.schoolnet.co.uk/GERunemployment.htm

Paper A, Section 3, Part 4, Source B:
The impact of the Great Depression on German politics.
Adapted from *Nazi Germany*, Stephen Lee, Pearson Education Limited

Paper B, Section 1, Part 2, Source A:
About the consequences of the Rough Wooing.
Adapted from *Scotland: A New History*, Michael Lynch, Pimlico.
Reproduced courtesy of Penguin Random House

Paper B, Section 1, Part 2, Source B:
Message from Mary to Elizabeth
Reprinted by permission of HarperCollins Publishers Ltd © 2004 John Guy

Paper B, Section 1, Part 4, Source A:
About migration from the Highlands and Lowlands of Scotland in the 19th century. Adapted from *Scottish Emigration: Going for Good* by Roger Hudson. History Today Volume: 62 Issue: 6 2012 (http://www.historytoday.com/rogerhudson/scottish-emigration-going-good)

Paper B, Section 1, Part 4, Source B:
Account of Irish sugar-workers in Greenock, 1836 from a Report on the State of the Irish Poor in Great Britain, Parliamentary Papers.
Adapted from Ireland in Schools website:
http://www.iisresource.org/Documents/Irish_In_Britain_Booklet_02.pdf

Paper B, Section 3, Part 2, Source A:
Describes the Tsar's government of Russia between 1905 and 1914.
Adapted from Heinemann *Scottish History for Standard Grade: Russia 1914–41*, Colin Bagnall, Pearson Education Limited

Paper B, Section 3, Part 2, Source B:
Describes the Tsar's government of Russia between 1905 and 1914.
Adapted from *Russia under the Bolshevik Regime*, Richard Pipes, Alfred Knopf Inc.
Reproduced by permission of Random House

Paper B, Section 3, Part 8, Source A:
About the Treaty of Versailles signed in June 1918
Adapted from the History Learning Site:
http://www.historylearningsite.co.uk/treaty_of_versailles.htm

Paper B, Section 3, Part 8, Source B:
About the reasons why Britain adopted a policy of Appeasement towards Germany in the 1930s.
Adapted from BBC Bitesize website: http://www.bbc.co.uk/bitesize/higher/history/roadwar/appease/revision/2/

MIX
Paper from responsible sources
FSC® C007454

ebook

To access the ebook version of this Revision Guide visit
www.collins.co.uk/ebooks
and follow the step-by-step instructions.

Contents

ANSWERS Check your answers to the practice test papers online:
www.collins.co.uk/pages/Scottish-curriculum-free-resources

Introduction

Complete Revision and Practice

This Complete **two-in-one Revision and Practice** book is designed to support you as students of National 5 History. It can be used either in the classroom, for regular study and homework, or for exam revision. By combining **a revision guide and two full sets of practice test papers**, this book includes everything you need to be fully familiar with the National 5 History exam. As well as including ALL the core course content with practice opportunities, there is comprehensive assignment and exam preparation advice with revision question and practice test paper answers provided online at www.collins.co.uk/pages/Scottish-curriculum-free-resources

About the revision guide

This guide is designed to help students achieve their potential in National 5 History. It should be used as part of the student's revision for the exam in terms of both content and skills.

The content is broken down into four sub-headings for each chapter and conforms to the SQA guidelines. This provides students with an easy-to-manage revision structure. The Exam skills section supports students when focusing on how to answer the exam questions. The Assignment section gives suggestions for possible topics for study.

About the practice papers

Hopefully, via history, you have learned a lot about what the world is like and how things have come to be the way they are. Above all I hope you have had fun with the past. However, now you are getting ready for your first major examination – you need to get in training! An athlete will prepare for a specific event in a major championship by practising the skills that are relevant to their event. You should take every opportunity to rehearse the skills that you will need in  the examination that forms the major part of the 'value added' element of the National 5 course. Some of these skills will overlap with the skills that you use in your assignment. For example, you need to know specific facts about your chosen topic; you need to organise those facts into an explanation, picking out the most important ones; you need to write all of that down in sentences that make sense on their own and all together. All of these skills will stand you in good stead in the examination. However, just as a sprinter would want to copy exactly the conditions under which they would run the 100 metres when preparing for the Olympics or Commonwealth Games, you should, as much as possible, attempt examination questions of the type that you will face in the summer. A sprinter would not train by running the marathon or playing golf! That is the purpose of the practice papers: to train and fine-tune your skills for success in the National 5 History examination.

Leckie
the education publisher
for Scotland

National 5
HISTORY

For SQA 2019 and beyond

Revision Guide

Andrew Baxby, Denise Dunlop,
Neil McLennan and Thom Sherrington

Mary, from the 'Rough Wooing' to becoming Queen of France, to 1559

Scottish society in the 1540s

Scotland in the sixteenth century was a dangerous place and people's lives were hard.

- Most people lived in townships in the countryside. Their lives were controlled by local landowners.
- There were a growing number of burghs, centres for craftsmen and traders. Royal burghs were granted the privilege of trading overseas.
- The monarchy governed with the help of the Privy Council and Parliament. The monarch was advised by the nobility, important churchmen, officials and representatives of the royal burghs.
- Monarchs depended on the support of the nobility. Nobles ruled regions on behalf of the monarch and helped keep the peace. Nobles were expected to gather men to fight for the monarch in times of war. Regents were chosen from the nobility when Scotland did not have an adult monarch.

TOP TIP

Sometimes it is helpful to link key points to visual triggers in order to remember them. Illustrate these four key points on Scottish society in the 1540s. Look at your drawing a week later. Can you remember the key points?

The Scottish Church in the 1540s

Religion played a very important part in people's lives but there was growing criticism of the Catholic Church.

- The Church was too rich and did not use its wealth to help the poor.
- Some churchmen led wealthy lifestyles.
- Some churchmen held several church positions and often did not do their work properly.
- Some monks and nuns did not lead holy lives.
- Kings and nobles bought Church positions for family members.
- The Church was criticised for selling indulgences.
- Fewer people attended church and churches were falling into disrepair.

Laws were introduced to encourage churchmen to learn to read and to preach more often and there were laws against the sale of Church positions. These attempts at reform were unsuccessful.

Scotland's relationship with England and France

In 1542 Mary, Queen of Scots succeeded to the throne. As she was too young to rule herself, James Hamilton, Earl of Arran was made Regent of Scotland. In 1554 Mary's French mother, Mary of Guise, became Regent. During these years both the English and the French tried to gain control of Scotland.

- **The Treaty of Greenwich** (1543) arranged for Mary to marry Henry VIII's son, Edward. Henry insisted that Mary be sent to England. He also wanted control of Scottish castles south of the Forth. He seized Scottish ships and demanded that Scotland put an end to the old alliance with France.

- Henry's demands resulted in the Scottish Parliament cancelling the Treaty of Greenwich. Henry sent armies to punish the Scots and capture Mary. The English invasions were called the '**Rough Wooing**'.

- The English attacks led to the **Treaty of Haddington** in 1548. Mary was to go to France for safety and would marry the French king's son, Francis.

- In 1558 Mary and Francis were married. In 1559, on his father's death, Francis became king of France and Mary became queen.

- Mary's dynastic position became stronger in 1558 on the accession of Elizabeth I. Many Catholics did not recognise Protestant Elizabeth as the true Queen of England. Mary was Elizabeth's closest living relation and heir.

Mary and her first husband, Francis II of France

Quick Test

1. How did the nobility support the monarchy in the sixteenth century?
2. What criticisms were made of the Catholic Church in the sixteenth century?
3. Why did the Scottish Parliament cancel the Treaty of Greenwich?
4. Why was Mary, Queen of Scots sent to France in 1548?

The Reformation in Scotland, 1560

The growth of Protestantism in Scotland

In the 1540s and 1550s Protestant ideas began to spread. People began to follow the ideas of Martin Luther, a German monk who criticised the Catholic Church. Martin Luther's ideas spread in a movement called the Reformation.

- People began to protest against the corruption of the Catholic Church in Scotland.
- Religious pamphlets from Europe and English translations of the Bible began to appear.
- Reformers such as George Wishart began to spread Protestant ideas.
- John Knox, one of Wishart's followers, gained support for the reformed Church. Knox was influenced by John Calvin, a follower of Martin Luther.
- Calvin believed people should live strict lives to save them from damnation and also believed church services should be simple and be held in plain churches.
- In 1557 some Protestant Scottish lords declared their intention to establish the Reformation in Scotland in a document called the 'First band of the Lords of the Congregation of Christ'. They became known as the Lords of the Congregation.

THINK POINT

Knox wrote a pamphlet called *The First Blast of the Trumpet Against the Monstrous Regiment of Women*. Knox referred to females as 'frail, weak, feeble and impatient creatures'. This attack was aimed at Mary of Guise and Mary Tudor of England. How do you think Mary, Queen of Scots and Elizabeth I of England felt about Knox's views on female rulers?

Rebellion against Mary of Guise

In 1559 there was a rising against Mary of Guise. The reasons for this were:

- Mary, Queen of Scots' marriage increased French influence over Scotland. The marriage treaty stated that Scotland was now part of France, a Catholic country.
- Mary of Guise had Protestant leaders executed.
- The death of Mary Tudor in 1558 and the accession of Elizabeth, a Protestant, to the throne of England, encouraged Protestant leaders in Scotland.

The Protestant rebellion was supported by Elizabeth I, while Mary of Guise received help from France. Fighting took place until the death of Mary of Guise in June 1560.

- The Treaty of Edinburgh in July 1560 agreed that both French and English forces were to withdraw from Scotland.
- The Scottish Parliament passed laws that led to Scotland becoming a Protestant country.

The Reformation after 1560

The regencies of Moray and Morton

The Protestant Reformation in Scotland developed under the regents who governed while James VI was too young to rule. In 1567 a law was passed stating that official positions were only to be held by Protestants. By 1574 most parishes had Protestant ministers and in 1579 Bibles began to be produced in Scotland. The Protestant Reformation was also strengthened after the defeat of the Queen's Lords in 1573 under Regent Morton.

Regent	Dates
Earl of Moray	1567–1570
Earl of Lennox	1570–1571
Earl of Mar	1571–1572
Earl of Morton	1572–1578

Young James VI

- Son of Mary, Queen of Scots and Henry Stuart, Lord Darnley. James was born on 19 June 1566 at Edinburgh Castle.
- Brought up Protestant, in the care of a strict tutor, George Buchanan.
- Became concerned by the power of the Protestant Church after being kidnapped by a group of Protestant lords led by Lord Ruthven (the Ruthven Raid, 1582).
- Wanted to have control of the Church through bishops; was opposed to presbyteries, i.e. church organisations made up of ministers and leading members of the church.

James VI as a boy

Andrew Melville and the development of Presbyterianism

The Protestant Reformation progressed further under the leadership of Andrew Melville. The Second Book of Discipline in 1578 contained his ideas for the Church in Scotland.

- Bishops should be abolished.
- The General Assembly should only consist of ministers and elders and not nobles or burgesses.
- The Kirk should have strict control of people's behaviour.

The Kirk of Scotland and the Black Acts

By 1581 the Kirk had planned for 13 presbyteries, which would give the Kirk control over appointing ministers and disciplinary matters. In essence, it seemed that the Kirk could be independent of the King and the influence of the nobility. This gave the Kirk influence and authority over members of the congregation. In 1584 after the Ruthven raids, James VI issued the Black Acts, to try and take control back from the Kirk. The Black Acts:

- Abolished presbyteries.
- Gave James the power to appoint bishops.
- No minister would be exempt from judgement of the ordinary courts.

In short, Royal Supremacy over the Kirk was established.

Quick Test

1. List five leading Protestant reformers mentioned in this chapter.
2. Who were the Lords of the Congregation?
3. Why was there a rising against Mary of Guise in 1559?
4. What was the Ruthven Raid?

Mary's reign, 1561–1567

Mary's return to Scotland

Mary, Queen of Scots returned to Scotland in August 1561. Most Scots welcomed Mary as Queen. She was young, beautiful and kind, and enjoyed light-hearted pastimes such as dancing at her court in Holyrood Palace in Edinburgh. Mary, however, was a Roman Catholic and faced problems in ruling a Protestant Scotland. These problems included:

- Some Scots opposed Mary as she was young and female.
- Some Scots resented Mary's French upbringing.
- Some Scots feared that Scotland would return to being Roman Catholic.

An etching depicting Mary's arrival in Leith, 1561

Mary also had to contend with Elizabeth I on the English throne. She was suspicious of Mary and worried she may lose her position as Queen of England to her. Catholics supported this and viewed Mary as the true Queen, not Elizabeth.

Mary's early reign

In the early years of her reign, Mary set up a successful government that included her Protestant half-brother James Stewart, who Mary made Earl of Moray. Mary travelled around Scotland to get to know her subjects and took action against nobles, such as the Earl of Huntly, who challenged her authority. Although she continued to practise the Catholic religion, Mary followed a tolerant religious policy.

- Mary allowed her Scottish subjects to follow the Protestant religion.
- Mary gave money to the Protestant Church.
- Mary did not allow priests to say Mass.
- Mary held several meetings with John Knox despite his criticism of her religion and lifestyle.

Mary's marriage

In 1565 Mary married Henry Stewart, Lord Darnley. This marriage caused problems for Mary and weakened her control of Scotland.

- Darnley was resented by many of the Scottish nobles. Mary's half-brother James, Earl of Moray, rebelled, which led to the Chaseabout Raid.
- Darnley's bad temper, drinking and long absences humiliated Mary.
- Darnley was involved in the murder of Mary's secretary, David Riccio, who was disliked due to his influence and friendship with Mary. He was also distrusted as he was a Catholic. Riccio was dragged from Mary's private rooms in Holyrood Palace and was stabbed 56 times with daggers and swords in front of Mary, who was pregnant at the time.

The murder of Riccio

Darnley's murder in 1567 ultimately led to Mary's downfall. Darnley's lodging house, Kirk O' Fields, was blown up by gunpowder and Darnley's body was found in the back garden. He had been suffocated. It was believed that a group of nobles including James Hepburn, Earl of Bothwell, and the Earl of Morton, were responsible. Mary's hurried marriage to Bothwell led to Mary being blamed for Darnley's murder. Some people believed Mary was already in a relationship with Bothwell and that together they had plotted to murder Darnley. Mary's enemies now thought she was unfit to govern.

TOP TIP

When looking at historical sources about Mary, Queen of Scots, consider the reliability of the evidence. Think about the authorship of the source. For example, sources written by John Knox, a Protestant leader, were biased against Mary.

Rebellion against Mary

- Some Scottish nobles rebelled. Mary surrendered to the rebels at Carberry Hill on 15 June 1567.

- Mary was captured and imprisoned in Loch Leven Castle.

- Mary was forced to abdicate and her 13-month-old son was crowned James VI. The Earl of Moray became Regent.

- Mary was imprisoned for ten and a half months but in May 1568 she managed to escape disguised as a servant with the help of her jailors.

- Mary raised an army at Hamilton but was defeated by the Earl of Moray's army on 13 May 1568, at the Battle of Langside.

- Mary fled to England in the hope that her cousin Elizabeth would help her.

Quick Test

1. What problems did Mary face when she returned to Scotland in 1561?

2. How did Mary show she was a strong ruler in the early years of her reign in Scotland?

3. Why was Riccio disliked by Darnley and the Scottish nobles?

4. Where was Mary imprisoned in Scotland after her surrender at Carberry Hill in June 1567?

Mary in England, 1567–1587

Mary's imprisonment

Mary escaped from her Scottish enemies but she did not receive help from Elizabeth. Instead Elizabeth had Mary imprisoned.

In 1568–1569 an enquiry was held to investigate Mary's involvement in Darnley's murder. The Earl of Moray produced a silver casket containing love letters Mary had allegedly written to Bothwell as evidence that they had plotted together to kill Darnley. The English nobles examining the letters could not decide if Mary was guilty or not. Elizabeth, however, saw Mary as a rival and kept Mary in captivity for almost 19 years. She was moved from one castle to another to prevent her supporters from plotting to free her.

Why did Mary's presence in England cause problems for Elizabeth?

- If Mary was sent back to Scotland, she might be executed by her Protestant enemies. Elizabeth would be acknowledging the right of subjects to rebel against their ruler.
- If Mary was sent abroad, Catholic rulers might use her as a focus to rally support for an attack against Protestant England.
- If Mary was allowed to live freely in England, she might try to seize the English throne. As Elizabeth was childless, she feared that Mary's supporters would try to kill her and put Mary on the English throne.
- Even if Mary remained imprisoned in England, she could still be a rallying point for English Catholics who believed that Mary, a Roman Catholic related to the English royal family, should be Queen of England. This became a real danger for Elizabeth in 1570 when the Pope declared Elizabeth was no longer England's rightful Queen.

Catholic plots

Mary's presence became an increasing threat to Elizabeth's position as Queen and to her safety, as Mary became the focus of Catholic plots to kill Elizabeth and to make Mary Queen of England. Mary knew little about many of the plots.

1569	The Northern Catholics	A group of Mary's supporters wanted Mary to succeed to the English throne and restore the Catholic religion.
1571	The Ridolfi Plot	Roberto Ridolfi, an Italian agent of the Pope, planned to use a Spanish army to free Mary and the Catholic Duke of Norfolk from the Tower of London. The plan involved Mary marrying Norfolk and becoming Queen of England.
1583	The Throckmorton Plot	A plan for a Spanish invasion of England.
1585	The Parry Plot	A plot to assassinate Elizabeth.
1586	The Babington Plot	Sir Anthony Babington, an English Catholic, plotted to free Mary, with Spanish help, murder Elizabeth and restore the Roman Catholic religion by placing Mary on the English throne.

However, Sir Francis Walsingham, one of Elizabeth's ministers, was appointed to find evidence against Mary. Mary's involvement in the Babington Plot provided the evidence that Mary was plotting against Elizabeth.

- Mary wrote to Babington agreeing to the plot.
- Unknown to Mary, a trap had been laid and all letters to and from Mary were being read by Walsingham.
- Mary was arrested and put on trial. Mary defended herself with dignity but was found guilty of treason and sentenced to death.

Mary's execution

Elizabeth hesitated to sign Mary's death warrant. Elizabeth was reluctant to kill another Queen and Mary was Elizabeth's cousin. On 1 February 1587 Elizabeth signed Mary's death warrant, which had been hidden among a pile of letters requiring her signature. Elizabeth later claimed she signed the letters quickly without reading them properly. On 8 February 1587 Mary was executed in the Great Hall of Fotheringhay Castle.

The execution of Mary

THINK POINT

How many years did Mary spend in France? In Scotland? In England? In which country did she spend most of her time? Is this surprising? If so, think of a reason.

Quick Test

1. What was produced by the Earl of Moray as evidence that Mary and Bothwell had planned Darnley's murder?
2. Why was Mary moved from castle to castle during her imprisonment in England?
3. What was the Babington Plot?
4. How did Elizabeth eventually sign Mary's death warrant?

Timeline

- Mary is born and becomes Queen of Scotland.
- The Scottish Parliament agrees and then rejects the Treaty of Greenwich.
- Treaty of Haddington. Mary leaves Scotland to live in France.
- Mary of Guise becomes Regent.
- Mary marries the Dauphin Francis.
- Scotland becomes a Protestant country.
- Mary returns to Scotland.
- Darnley is murdered. Mary marries James, the Earl of Bothwell.
- Mary escapes from Loch Leven Castle and flees to England. Mary is imprisoned in England.
- Mary is executed at Fotheringhay Castle.

Biographies

Henry Stewart, Lord Darnley (1545–1567)

Darnley and Mary were married in July 1565. He was Mary's cousin and, like Mary, had a claim to the English throne. Darnley, however, was not a good husband to Mary and his ambitions to be crowned King of Scotland made him many enemies. He was murdered in February 1567.

James Hepburn, Earl of Bothwell (1534–1578)

Bothwell and Mary were married in May 1567. The marriage led to an uprising by the Scottish nobles who believed Bothwell was guilty of Darnley's murder. After the surrender of Mary's army at Carberry Hill, Bothwell fled to Scandinavia in the hope of raising support for Mary but was imprisoned in Denmark and died in captivity in 1578.

John Knox (1514–1572)

In 1547 John Knox was sent to row in the French galleys as a punishment for joining the murderers of Cardinal Beaton, in St Andrew's castle. After his release, Knox studied Protestant ideas on the Continent before returning to Scotland in 1559. In 1560 his Book of Discipline outlined his ideas for the reformed Church in Scotland.

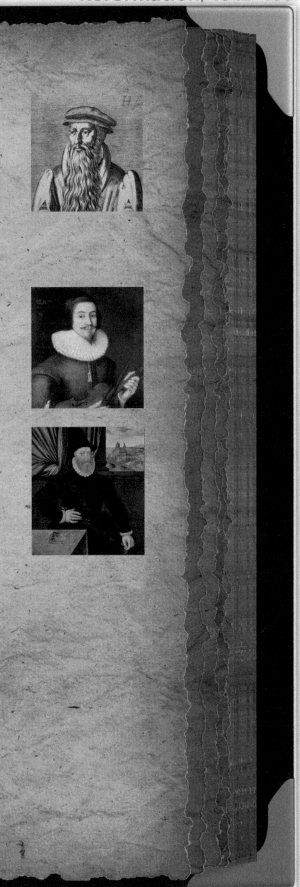

David Riccio (1533–1566)

David Riccio came to Scotland in 1561 and became Mary's secretary in 1564. Mary and Riccio shared a love of music and poetry but their close friendship led to his murder by a group of Scottish nobles in March 1566.

James Douglas, Earl of Morton (1516–1581)

James Douglas became Regent in 1572. He ended the conflict with Mary's supporters. In 1580 he was arrested for his involvement in Darnley's murder and executed in Edinburgh in 1581. He was beheaded on the maiden, a guillotine he himself had introduced into Scotland.

Immigration to Scotland

Why did immigrants come to Scotland?

From 1830 to 1939, Scotland witnessed the arrival of immigrants from across Europe. Each arrived for a variety of reasons. These can be divided into 'push' and 'pull' factors.

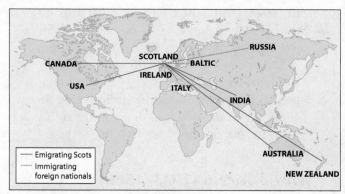

Immigration and emigration, to 1939

Push	Pull
High unemployment rates in Europe and Ireland.	Job opportunities created by the industrial revolution.
Wages were often very low in these areas.	Scotland offered higher wages for the immigrants.
Religious and political persecution (especially Jews and Catholics from eastern Europe). Many Jews fled central Europe to escape the Nazis.	Scotland was seen as a place where different religious practices were more accepted, and democracy ruled.
The potato famine in Ireland forced people to leave due to the threat of starvation.	Scotland was near to Ireland and offered work and food to the hungry Irish workers.
	Scotland was also a stop on the way to America (especially for eastern Europeans).

Where did the immigrants settle?

TOP TIP

Emigration = leaving (remember the 'E' in exit). **I**mmigration = arriving (remember the 'I' in into). Often pull factors and push factors are closely related. For example, low wages are a push factor and better wages are a pull factor.

In general, immigrants settled in the central belt, where the jobs were.

Irish immigrants arrived desperately seeking employment and often worked as navvies, building the canals, railways and roads. Glasgow and Dundee became swamped with Irish immigrants.

Jewish immigrants tended to settle on the south side of Glasgow, working as professionals (lawyers, accountants, bankers). Their religious practices often seemed bizarre to the native Scots and they found it difficult to integrate into Scottish society.

In general, Jews were seen as less of an economic threat than the Irish, as unemployment was low in the Jewish community.

Italians generally came to escape the crushing poverty in Italy's rural communities. Many used Scotland as a stop-off on the way to America. They set up ice cream parlours and coffee shops. Italians faced hostility when Mussolini sided with Hitler in the Second World War.

An ice cream parlour, Edinburgh, 1907

Lithuanians also came to Scotland. Many left to avoid being drafted into the Russian army or were fleeing persecution under the policy of Russification, which disallowed books to be written or read in the Lithuanian language. Some think the Lithuanians were sometimes tricked into thinking they were in America when they were in fact in Scotland. After docking at the Port of Leith, many found jobs in mining in Newtongrange in Midlothian, or in the ironworks of Lanarkshire.

What was the impact of Empire on Scotland?

- There were opportunities to work for the Colonial Government or army, which helped some become very rich.
- The opportunities for Scots to emigrate to far-flung places helped to relieve some of the problems at home. There was less pressure on the scarce farmland of the western Highlands, and widespread starvation was avoided.
- Unemployment in the towns and cities was lessened.
- Profits made by Scottish businessmen in the Empire helped Glasgow's city fathers to supply clean water, affordable gas, public parks and better sewerage.
- New materials and foodstuffs arrived. Glasgow became the 'second city of the Empire' with ships built there going all over the world. Trains built in Scotland were running on the new lines in Canada, India and New Zealand. Jute from India gave Dundee factories material to work with.

Politically, the Empire arguably gave Scotland a higher profile in the world, and the export of 'Scottishness' to many parts of the Empire gives an idea of the influence that the Empire had on Scotland.

However, some have argued that this emigration led to a 'brain drain'. Many of the finest businessmen and thinkers left Scotland to make their fortunes in the Empire.

Quick Test

1. List three push and three pull factors for migration to Scotland.
2. Why were Jewish immigrants seen as less of a threat than other immigrants?
3. Why did Jewish immigration increase in the 1930s?
4. What was the name given to Glasgow at the height of the Empire?

Experience of immigrants, 1830s–1939

Where did the immigrants live and work?

Many of the immigrants to Scotland lived in the poorest conditions. They worked in the poorest paid jobs and so could not afford better accommodation.

They were often employed in dangerous, dirty work such as in factories or coal mines. Due to their willingness to work for low wages, they were accused of stealing jobs as many employers would sack well-paid Scots and employ low-paid immigrants.

A miner at Camp Colliery, Motherwell, circa 1890

Irish immigration

TOP TIP

Sectarianism (religious tension) was often a symptom of the economic problems and high unemployment rate at the time. Tension increased at times of hardship.

In Scotland, the Protestant Irish tended to integrate well into all areas of society, whereas Catholics remained on the margins of society. There was racial/sectarian tension in certain areas of Scotland, and this increased at times of unemployment. The experiences of the Protestant Irish and Catholic Irish differed in various ways:

Catholics	Protestants
Made up about 75% of all Irish immigrants.	Made up about 25% of all Irish immigrants.
Had more in common with the Scottish Highlanders and spoke Gaelic.	Had more in common with the Scottish Lowlanders and spoke English.
Religion marked them out as very different from the establishment.	Formed Orange Lodges in order to preserve their way of life and to show their rejection of the Catholic religion.
To begin with, they integrated well by marrying Scots, changing surnames and religion.	Integrated more easily as they had more in common politically, and they often had Scottish sounding surnames.
Found it difficult to find employment in certain areas – were sometimes paid less than Protestants.	Often found it easier to gain employment.

As numbers of Catholic immigrants grew, so did the native Scots' resentment. Catholics tended to remain in their own communities and were increasingly blamed for the high unemployment. Many were happy to work for low wages and live in very poor conditions. This made them easy targets to blame for the ever-worsening living conditions in Scotland's growing towns. A common myth was that the Irish Catholics were coming to Scotland in order to seek Poor Relief.

In the 1920s there was significant violence between Catholics and Protestants in Glasgow and other parts of Scotland. However, tension in Scotland should not be exaggerated, as throughout the nineteenth century there are examples of co-operation, such as in the building of the canals, railways and ships. During the First World War, Catholics and Protestants fought side-by-side in the British Forces.

What was the impact of Irish immigration on Scotland?

Irish immigration had a very mixed impact on Scotland.

- The Irish navvies helped establish Scotland's transport infrastructure, building roads, railways and canals. For example, in 1890 the Glasgow subway was tunnelled using largely Irish labourers.
- The arrival of a large (and cheap) workforce from Ireland did help boost the economy, even if Scots workers were unemployed as a result.
- The arrival of thousands of Irish Catholics led to the establishment of a separate system of Catholic schools.
- Sports teams were set up as a focus for young immigrant men; for example, Celtic, Hibernian and Dundee Hibernian (now Dundee United) football clubs were founded.
- Politically, Irish workers played a large role in the rise of the Labour Party.

Opening of the Glasgow subway, 1896

Quick Test

1. Why were Irish Catholic immigrants often unpopular in Scotland?
2. Why were Protestants accepted more quickly?
3. Give two lasting impacts of Catholic immigration.
4. What did Irish navvies help to build?

Scottish emigration, 1830s–1939

While there were large numbers arriving in Scotland at this time, there was also significant **emigration** *from* Scotland.

Poverty was a key factor in pushing people from Scotland. We know this as emigration peaked in the 1850s, 1870s, early 1900s and between the World Wars. These coincided with periods of significant economic hardship.

THINK POINT

Trotsky said that 'War is the locomotive of history'. What do you think he meant by this? In this case it is the First World War. Why do you think war brings about change?

Why did Scots leave?

Jobs

In the 1870s farming experienced a downturn due to foreign competition. Thousands lost their jobs and they and their families went hungry. In the 1900s fishing was also hit hard by foreign competition. The slump after the First World War and the Great Depression saw heavy industry go into decline, forcing those in the cities to leave and find work.

Highland Clearances

Some were forced from the land due to the Highland Clearances. The growth in population of the nineteenth century meant that the land could not feed the people living there. The crofts were getting smaller and rents were increasing drastically. Landlords realised they could make more money from the land by grazing sheep (especially when the value of wool

An evicted family in Lochmaddy, 1895

rose) and from creating shooting estates. To make matters worse, the potato famine of 1846 left 150 000 people at risk of starvation.

Thus, people were keen to move away from the poor conditions of the Highlands, but they were also forced to move by ruthless landlords.

The Church

Some were encouraged to move abroad by the opportunities of missionary work. The Presbyterian Church gave Scots clergy the opportunity to venture to exciting places in the Empire. They were supported financially to set up missions in order to convert native people and other migrants to Christianity. Missionaries, such as Mary Slessor (Nigeria), Alexander Duff (India) and William Chalmers Burns (China) continued to spread the Scottish Presbyterian message far and wide and encouraged others to follow.

Other organisations

Others were encouraged to move by the many emigration societies and the Colonial Government. Emigration societies offered support to (mostly skilled) workers in terms of transport costs and finding employment. This was especially common in Canada. They advertised for workers and organised everything for the migrant, even providing land for farming in the country of destination.

The Colonial Land and Emigration Commissioners gave grants and loans to support emigrants in the New World. After the Empire Settlement Act of 1922, the government gave money to countries of the Empire in order to encourage emigration. The New Zealand and Australian governments offered free travel for those working in domestic service.

The attraction of the New World

Some moved due to the pull of the 'New World', i.e. Canada, Australia, New Zealand and the USA. Wages tended to be higher, there was more land to farm and more jobs to be had in the cities. They could start again in a country with better farmland and more freedom. The land tended to be very cheap and many Scots set up huge plantations and ranches. Others moved in order to join family already successfully established. Others still were lured away from the sectarian problems at home by the idea of religious freedom.

A group of Scots leaving for Canada, 1925

Thus, Scots moved for a wide variety of reasons; some were pushed, others were pulled.

Quick Test

1. Why did the Highland Clearances happen?
2. What was the role of the Church in Scottish emigration?
3. Why is 1922 important to the story?
4. Where is the New World?

Experience of Scots abroad, 1830s–1939

Where did Scots settle?

Scots moved to a variety of locations across the globe including England, but the most common destinations were Canada, Australia, New Zealand and India. Even today, the Scottish influence can be seen in these countries.

Canada

More Scots went to Canada than anywhere else before 1847. They proved very successful in industry, dominating textiles, paper, sugar, oil, iron, coal, steel, furniture making, the fur trade and banking. They also had a huge influence on culture. Scots formed Burns clubs and Caledonian societies, and introduced rugby, football and curling. They played a huge role in politics, and Scots were key in making sure that Canada's main language was English and not French. John A Macdonald (from Glasgow) was Canada's first Prime Minister and founded the Canadian Mounted Police. There are lots of Scottish place names to this day (e.g. Dundee, Leith, Glasgow, Inverness, Stirling).

A pipe band in Vancouver, 2013

Australia

Scots were attracted to Australia in large numbers from 1851 with the discovery of gold. Scots were mostly successful in industries such as the wool trade, coal mining, farming, banking and construction.

The Presbyterian Church had a very strong hold in Australia. This was linked closely with the development of the education system.

However, Scots had a very negative impact on native societies, exemplified by the Warrigal Creek massacre. Aboriginal children were forcibly removed from their parents to be educated and westernised.

New Zealand

The New Zealand tourist board boasts that 'you'll find a Scottish presence everywhere in New Zealand life'. It was a popular destination for Scots (especially Otago), with a similar climate and terrain. Farming was the main industry for Scots in New Zealand, although they played an important role in banking, gold prospecting and skilled trades like shipbuilding. Caledonian societies were very common, and Gaelic was the first language in some areas until the 1880s. Highland gatherings and St Andrew's societies flourished. Countless names show the impact of Scots (e.g. Clyde, Ben Nevis, Aviemore).

Again, the strong Presbyterian influence was exported. The 'Scotch Church' is still powerful to this day in Otago.

> ### DID YOU KNOW?
> The first recorded European settler in New Zealand was Scottish. His name was George Bruce. Use the internet to research more about some of these key Scots. Make a profile of each one, looking at where they came from, why they emigrated and what they achieved.

India

The British East India Company gave Scots the opportunity to trade with India, and they took full advantage. They flourished in the jute trade and Thomas Lipton was a shining example of the spirit of the Scots that ventured to this new land. He was a grocer and tea importer, who revolutionised tea drinking in Britain by making it cheaper and more fashionable.

Seven of the 12 viceroys of India were Scots, and they played crucial roles in all areas of government in the colony. They built railways, increased civil rights and encouraged female education. The relationship with native societies was generally more positive than elsewhere, although the Colonial Government did little to aid famine and suffering.

Lipton's tea being carried on elephants

Quick Test

1. How do we know that the impact of Scots in Canada was great and lasting?
2. Why did so many Scots go to Australia after 1851?
3. Where was the biggest Scottish settlement in New Zealand?
4. What did Thomas Lipton do?

Timeline

- Mechanical spinning makes Dundee centre of world jute trade.
- Start of potato famine in Ireland.
- Potato famine affects the Highlands of Scotland.
- Gold discovered in Australia.
- India becomes a British colony.
- British North America formed (modern day Canada).
- Hibernian Football Club formed by Irish born football enthusiasts.
- Modern day Australia formed as a Dominion in the British Empire.
- New Zealand becomes a Dominion in the British Empire.
- Government offers money to colonies to encourage emigration (Empire Settlement Act).

Biographies

Andrew Carnegie (1835–1919)

Born in Dunfermline, Carnegie made his name in America. His family emigrated to Pennsylvania in 1848, where he worked in a factory. He made his fortune in the railway expansion of the 1860s and 1870s. In the 1880s Carnegie formed steel companies that made him incredibly wealthy. His company was ultimately bought out for a vast sum of money. He spent his retirement funding projects in America, Scotland and elsewhere, including giving $10 million to Scotland's universities.

John Buchan, 1st Baron Tweedsmuir (1875–1940)

Brought up in Kirkaldy in Fife, Buchan led a fairly privileged life. He was well-educated and served in the diplomatic service after university. He went on to fight in the First World War and to become Governor General of Canada in 1935. He was also a famous author (*The Thirty-Nine Steps* is his most famous work) and was a strong critic of the policy of appeasement in the 1930s.

Andrew Fisher (1862–1928)

Fisher was born in East Ayrshire and worked in a coal mine from age 10. When he lost his job in 1885 he decided to emigrate to Australia. There he again worked in mines and was elected as an MP for the Labour Party. He went on to be Prime Minister of Australia three times between 1908 and 1915. He was also High Commissioner to the UK between 1916 and 1921. He died in London of severe influenza in 1928. He was also suffering from dementia.

John Muir (1838–1914)

Born near Dunbar in East Lothian, Muir is considered the 'Father of the National Parks' in America. He is credited with preserving Yosemite and Sequoia National Parks. His name is given to numerous important places, but it is the 211-mile hiking trail in the Sierra Nevada mountain range in California that is probably the best-known. The John Muir award in the UK is given to those that complete wilderness and conservation challenges.

Thomas Lipton (1850–1931)

Tommy Lipton grew up in Glasgow's Gorbals area. He left school at 10, and set up his first market stall in 1870. He set up a business exporting tea from India and Ceylon (now Sri Lanka) in the 1890s. Lipton's plan was to reduce its cost and make it affordable for the average British shopper. His other novel idea was to begin packaging it, instead of selling it loose from the chest. He was knighted by Queen Victoria in 1898.

Scots on the Western Front

In 1914 war broke out between the Triple Alliance (Germany, Austria-Hungary, Italy) and the Triple Entente (Britain, France, Russia). Scots fought predominantly on the 'Western Front', which ran from the Belgian North Sea coast to the Franco-Swiss border.

TOP TIP

Research the involvement of Scots in major battles of the First World War. 30 000 Scottish troops fought at the battle of Loos and five soldiers were later awarded the Victoria Cross for bravery.

Why did so many Scots join the army?

Scots volunteered in massive numbers and many lied about their age to do so. As well as patriotism, there were other reasons for joining up:

Excitement	The war was portrayed as exciting and glamorous. The prevailing attitude was that it 'would be over by Christmas', so volunteers did not expect a long period of service.
Propaganda	Accusations of German atrocities in Belgium, e.g. rape of nuns, murder of babies and torture of civilians, were accepted as truth.
Football supporters	Thirteen players from the team 'Heart of Midlothian' volunteered to fight, which encouraged hundreds of supporters and other teams to follow suit.
Employment and wages	The average army pay of nine or ten shillings a week was more than many Scots were paid in civilian life.

Life in the trenches

Conditions in the trenches were horrific.

- Men often had to stand in mud up to their ankles. This led to diseases such as trench foot.
- Pests such as rats and lice were everywhere.
- Food was not nutritious (e.g. canned stew). Fresh fruit and vegetables were rare.
- Constant shellfire led to 'shell shock'.
- The danger of death was always close. Artillery fire was constant and enemy snipers could easily shoot men who stuck their heads above the parapet.

Conditions in the trenches could be terrible, with mud a particular problem.

New technology

The war evolved into a stalemate, so both sides dug trenches to defend their positions. This meant that traditional tactics such as the cavalry charge became obsolete. New technology was important in trying to break the stalemate.

Artillery	• Most widely used method of attack was heavy artillery fire. • Huge guns fired shells packed with explosives towards the enemy lines.
Gas	• Three main gases were used: mustard, chlorine and phosgene. • Effects varied from severe skin irritation to suffocation and death. • Proved to be unreliable because wind could blow it back towards the side it had come from; gas masks were developed to counter the effects.
Tanks	• Developed to advance into enemy territory, break through enemy barbed wire and clear the way for infantry to follow. • First used at the Battle of the Somme. • Often broke down and became stuck in the mud.
Machine guns	• The ultimate defensive weapon. • Two or three machine gunners could fire hundreds of rounds a minute into advancing enemy infantry.
Aircraft	• Initially used for reconnaissance missions over enemy territory. • Were later developed with machine guns attached to fire upon enemy aircraft.

Military tactics

British troops have been described as 'Lions led by donkeys' because, although they displayed great courage, the strategy of the British generals led to massive casualties.

The main tactic was to bombard the enemy with artillery fire and then send troops 'over the top' towards enemy lines. The German machine guns, however, easily slaughtered the advancing British troops. The Scottish General Douglas Haig, Commander of the British forces during the war, has been heavily criticised for persisting with this tactic when it was so expensive in human life. Others argue that his strategy exhausted the German army and was ultimately responsible for the British victory.

Quick Test

1. Why did so many Scots volunteer for the army?
2. Why did new technology play such an important role in the war?
3. What was the main tactic employed by the British forces?
4. Who led the British forces in the war?

Domestic impact of war: society and culture

The First World War has been described as a 'total war' because its effects were felt in the homes and workplaces of Britain and Scotland, not just on the battlefield.

Defence of the Realm Act (DORA)

The First World War led to the passing of the Defence of the Realm Act in 1914. This gave the government wide-ranging powers to legislate on people's lives to ensure the successful continuation of the war effort.

- Pub opening hours were cut and the strength of beer was weakened to ensure high production levels in industrial areas.
- DORA gave the government the power to take over factories and turn them into munitions works.
- It allowed the government to censor the press to avoid stories that they thought might damage public morale.

Before DORA the philosophy of successive governments had been *'laissez-faire'*, i.e. they did not want to interfere in people's lives. With the passing of DORA, however, the government actively legislated on many aspects of public life.

> **DID YOU KNOW?**
>
> Pub opening hours were enforced in areas near munitions factories. Previously pubs had opened at 5am and workers would stop in before work. Disasters caused by drunkenness were a serious concern!

Rationing

In 1914 Britain relied on imports for the majority of its food. Germany launched submarine attacks on British merchant ships to reduce Britain to the point of starvation. By 1917 there were food shortages, which led to rising prices and panic buying. This led to the introduction of rationing on items such as sugar, meat and butter. Some items remained rationed until 1920.

Changing role of women

The war is often seen as a turning point in the role of women in British society.

- As men left for the front, women filled the gaps in the workforce.
- Women worked on buses, as typists, in the civil service and in the police.
- Over 30 000 women worked in the munitions industry in Scotland and thousands joined the Women's Land Army, which helped to sustain agriculture.

It is argued that by proving that they could be relied upon to work, they also proved that they could be trusted to vote and play a prominent role in society.

However, at the end of the war most women lost their jobs and were expected to return to their pre-war roles. It can thus be argued that the role of the war in changing the role of women in society has been exaggerated.

Propaganda

Propaganda was political advertising used by the government to influence the way people thought about the war. The huge volume of propaganda meant that the war infiltrated every aspect of public life. It was used to:

- encourage Scots to enlist
- encourage Scots to ration food
- boost morale and increase public support for the war.

Conscription

After the initial rush of volunteers had waned, the government was forced to introduce conscription to ensure army numbers remained adequate. Conscription meant that men were forced to join the army by law. In January 1916 the Military Service Act introduced conscription for single men aged 18–40. This was extended to married men in March 1916 and men up to 50 years old in 1918.

Conscientious objectors

Some men claimed they could not fight because they objected to the war on the grounds of conscience, citing their religious or political beliefs. 16 000 men in total were classified as conscientious objectors (COs or Conchies). Most COs agreed to do some sort of work to help the war effort, for example farm work, but absolutists refused to do anything to help the war effort and were sentenced to hard labour. One labour camp was situated in Dyce, on the outskirts of Aberdeen, and the men were forced to work in a granite quarry.

Casualties and deaths

The true number of Scots killed in the First World War will never be known. The official number given was 75 000, but some claim that a more accurate figure may be closer to 150 000. What is not debated is that almost every community in Scotland suffered devastating losses and a whole generation of men was lost.

Scotland also suffered disproportionately when compared with the rest of the UK. Of the 557 000 Scots who enlisted in all services, 26.4% lost their lives. In comparison, the rest of the British army was 11.8%.

Quick Test

1. What is a 'total war'?
2. What role did women play during the war?
3. What is propaganda?
4. On what grounds did conscientious objectors refuse to fight in the war?

Domestic impact of war: industry and economy

As well as having a major impact on the society and culture of Scotland, the Great War also impacted greatly on industry and the economy. Prior to the war the traditional heavy industries of shipbuilding, mining and metalwork were in decline. This was reversed during the war and unemployment virtually disappeared. Once peace was achieved, however, the old problems returned, unemployment rose and the economy suffered.

War work

Several industries were boosted thanks to the war. The Royal Navy took control of the main shipbuilding firms on the Clyde. Increased demand for ships boosted employment in the area. The jute industry in Dundee also thrived. Jute was used to make cloth for sandbags, which were in heavy demand to line the walls of the trenches. As the German naval blockade took effect and food imports became scarce, Scottish agriculture increased to meet the shortfall. Many Scots found employment in munitions factories, which kept the army supplied with weapons and shells.

The cordite explosive factory at Gretna provided employment for over 9000 women during World War I.

Reserved occupations

Under the 1916 Military Service Act one of the grounds for exemption was: 'If it is expedient in the national interests that (a man) should be engaged in other work, or, if he is being educated or trained for any other work, that he should continue.' This meant that men employed in industries essential to the war effort such as coal mining, shipbuilding and munitions were able to apply for exemption from service. There was no specified list of occupations, however – local tribunals decided each case individually.

Post-war decline of heavy industry

Unfortunately the boom that heavy industries experienced during the war did not last and in the post-war period there was a rise in unemployment and a fall in the economy.

One of the main reasons for this was that the war created a huge demand for ships, coal, metal, munitions and other essential items. Once the war ended there was no longer a need to support the war effort so these orders disappeared.

Shipbuilding was once a major employer in Glasgow but it, along with many other heavy industries, declined in the 1920s.

Furthermore, during the four years of the war Britain's trading partners were forced to look elsewhere for suppliers. Britain's traditional industries such as textiles, coal mining, steel and iron production now faced many global competitors. Post-war British exports fell by 20%. Scotland, which relied heavily on traditional industries for employment, was badly affected by this depression.

Fishing and agriculture

Scotland had a profitable fishing business before the war. However, during the war the industry declined as it lost her buyers from Germany, Russia and Poland. Fishing was restricted from fear of attack by German U-boats. As a result, fish was rationed in 1917. After the war, the decline continued as custom had already moved elsewhere and it was hard to recover old trading relationships. On the other hand, agriculture prospered during WW1. Wages rose by 150% for some farmers, and skilled ploughmen could double their wages. The demand for wool for uniforms increased and the cost of a sheep rose by 60%. After the war, technological improvements replaced people, subsidies ended and prices for farmed goods fell by 25%.

New industry in the 1920s

There was some growth of new industries in Britain in the 1920s. The motor industry, chemical industry and electric industry all grew during this time. However, these industries tended to be based in the Midlands or in the south of England and so did not benefit Scots, who found themselves unemployed due to the post-war depression. Many Scots were forced to emigrate to find work abroad.

THINK POINT

The First World War had a massive impact on society in Scotland, Britain and the whole world. Create a mind map showing all of the changes and events that it can be said to have had a direct impact upon. Start off by using the notes from this chapter, but then think about all of the other topics you have studied in History and add them too.

Quick Test

1.   What was the effect of the outbreak of war on the Scottish economy?
2.   Which industries received a boost from the war?
3.   Why did the economy decline after the war?
4.   Why did the new industries of the 1920s not benefit Scots?

Domestic impact of war: politics

Campaigns for women's suffrage

Prior to the war, the peaceful suffragists and the militant suffragettes had been campaigning for the right of women to vote. When war broke out, however, both groups suspended their campaigns and supported the war effort. The suffragettes had been very active in Scotland, but postponed their campaigns at the outset of war.

Extension of the franchise

- In 1914 only 60% of men over the age of 21, and no women, could vote.
- In 1918 the Representation of the People Act enfranchised all men over the age of 21 (19 if they had fought in active service) and 'respectable' women over the age of 30.
- The act gave the vote to 21 million extra people in Britain; 8·4 million were women.
- Many women saw this as a victory, but others were dissatisfied with the continued inequality. It was not until 1928 that women were granted the vote on an equal basis.

Rent strikes

Industrial areas in Scotland, especially around Glasgow, experienced a large increase in population as people moved there for work. This led to an increased demand for housing. Landlords capitalised on this increased demand by raising rents and evicting those who could not pay in favour of those that could. Many of those affected were women whose men were away fighting.

- In 1915 the Glasgow Housing Association was formed and began protesting against the unfair and expensive rents.
- The rent strikes were led by women. The leadership of Mary Barbour and Helen Crawfurd was essential to the success of this movement.
- Eventually 25 000 workers from all over Scotland went on strike, threatening major disruption to the war effort.
- The Rent Restriction Act, which froze rents at 1914 levels, was eventually passed.

Glasgow became known as 'Red Clydeside' because of the amount of political and industrial unrest. Politicians were genuinely scared that a socialist revolution could occur and in 1919 even sent army tanks to disperse protestors in George Square.

Crowds of striking workers gathered in George Square in 1919.

Homes for heroes

David Lloyd George promised that returning soldiers would have clean and sanitary homes ('Homes for heroes'). This idea came to mean more than a home to live in, but also a right to a better standard of living. The 1919 Housing Act promised funding for 500 000 homes. Unfortunately, the unemployment and economic hardship of the 1920s made providing all of these houses impossible and only 213 000 were built.

Further acts passed in the inter-war years, however, meant that in total 1·1 million homes were built by local housing associations.

Quick Test

1. What was the impact of DORA?
2. Why did living conditions decline in Glasgow during the war?
3. What political changes occurred after the war ended?
4. How many new homes were built after the war?

Timeline

August 1914 – Britain declares war on Germany.

August 1914 – Defence of the Realm Act (DORA) passed.

September 1915 – First day of the Battle of Loos, in which 30 000 Scots fought.

December 1915 – Douglas Haig appointed Commander in Chief of the British forces.

January 1916 – Conscription introduced in Britain (Military Service Act).

July 1916 – First day of the Battle of the Somme. Britain suffered 60 000 casualties. This remains the worst day in the history of the British Army.

December 1916 – David Lloyd George becomes Prime Minister.

February 1918 – Representation of the People Act passed.

November 1918 – Armistice signed officially ending the First World War

Biographies

Sir Douglas Haig (1861–1928)

Born in Edinburgh, Haig was appointed Commander in Chief of the British forces in 1915. His tactics have been blamed for the huge casualty rates among British soldiers, particularly at the Battle of the Somme, where the British Army suffered 60 000 casualties on the first day of fighting alone. In his retirement he set up and devoted his life to the Royal British Legion, which cares for ex-servicemen.

David Lloyd George (1863–1945)

A prominent Liberal politician, Lloyd George became Prime Minister in 1916 and held that post until 1922. Brought up in a working-class family in Wales, he was an influential social reformer. During the war it is even said he insisted the Royal Family use candles instead of electric lights during banquets to save power for the war effort.

Millicent Fawcett (1847–1929)

Leader of the National Union of Women's Suffrage Societies, otherwise known as the 'suffragists'. The suffragists believed in 'peaceful persuasion' and campaigned for the right to vote for women by holding rallies, publishing pamphlets and working with politicians. In 1914 she called off the suffrage campaign and encouraged women to contribute to the war effort.

Emmeline Pankhurst (1858–1928)

Along with her two daughters, Christabel and Sylvia, Emmeline Pankhurst was the founder and leader of the Women's Social and Political Union, otherwise known as the 'suffragettes'. Like the suffragists, the suffragettes wanted votes for women, but they favoured using militant protests to achieve their aims. At the outbreak of war they too postponed their campaigns and encouraged men to enlist and women to serve the war effort.

Mary Barbour (1875–1958)

Mary Barbour was a political activist and local councillor in Glasgow who was the main organiser of the rent strikes in Govan in 1915. She organised protestors to refuse to pay rent increases and resist evictions. Her followers became known as 'Mrs Barbour's Army'.

John Maclean (1879–1923)

A Scottish school teacher and revolutionary socialist, John Maclean was one of the leading figures of Red Clydeside. He protested vehemently against the First World War and was imprisoned many times. His actions during Red Clydeside made him a hero in Russia, where he even appeared on postage stamps.

The triangular trade

The nature of the slave trade

Slavery is thousands of years old and the buying and selling of slaves had been taking place in Africa for hundreds of years. The slave trade of the eighteenth century, however, was a new kind of slavery.

Reasons why the slave trade was different	Evidence
The Atlantic slave trade was on a much larger scale than ever before.	Millions of African people were transported across the Atlantic as slaves.
The slave trade was racist.	Only African people were captured and sold into slavery for life.
Slaves became the property of slave owners.	Slaves were regarded as goods rather than as people. Few slaves were given their freedom. The children of slaves also became slaves.
The slave trade was a cruel form of slavery.	Slaves were ill-treated and kept in inhuman conditions. The law allowed a slave owner to beat a slave to death.

The slave trade expanded after many European countries set up colonies in the New World of the Americas. Britain played a major part in the Atlantic slave trade between 1770 and 1807.

The organisation of the slave trade

The trading system known as the **triangular trade** started in Europe and often involved three separate voyages:

Stage One: Outward Passage

In the first stage, ships sailed from a port such as Liverpool, Bristol or London to the coast of West Africa loaded with goods such as guns, alcohol, pots and pans and textiles to exchange for captured Africans. Industries supplying the slave traders, shipbuilding and the direct involvement in trading slaves made many individuals very wealthy in ports such as Liverpool and Bristol.

When the slave ships arrived on the African coast, British merchants would trade for slaves. Captured Africans, marched to the coast by African traders, were imprisoned in slave forts called 'factories' until the arrival of the slave ships.

- The slave trade had a devastating effect on West Africa. Europeans encouraged African states to go to war with one another so there would be more prisoners of war to sell as slaves. The population declined and traditional ways of life disappeared.

- Some African states such as the Dahomey and the Ashanti became very powerful due to their participation in the slave trade.

Stage Two: Middle Passage

The second stage was the transportation of enslaved Africans across the Atlantic Ocean to the Americas. This stage is known as the **Middle Passage**.

For most slaves the Middle Passage was an unbearable and brutal experience. Slaves were tightly packed and chained below deck in filthy, unsanitary conditions. Many slaves died from disease.

At the end of the Middle Passage, slaves were cleaned and made to look younger and healthier to make them more profitable. The slaves were then sold to plantation owners at auctions or 'scrambles'.

Stage Three: Inward Passage

The third stage was the journey back to Europe with plantation-grown goods, such as rum, tobacco, coffee, sugar, molasses and cotton bought from the profits of selling African slaves to the plantation owners. The raw materials would be turned into manufactured goods in Britain and then sold for large profits in Europe.

The triangular trade could take almost a year from start to finish. There were many risks but large profits could be made at each point of the triangular trade.

> **TOP TIP**
>
> Atlantic slave trade journeys often had three parts which made a triangular shape, linking three continents – Europe, Africa and the Americas – it was commonly called the 'triangular trade'. But not all slave voyages were triangular; some slave traders made single voyages.

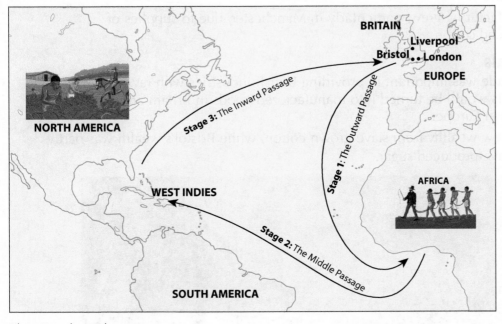

The triangular trade

Quick Test

1. What was new about the slave trade of the eighteenth century?
2. Describe conditions for slaves during the Middle Passage.
3. What were the three destinations in the triangular trade?
4. What goods were transported in the triangular trade?

Britain and the Caribbean

The effects of the Atlantic slave trade on Britain

The Atlantic slave trade had a major impact on Britain's economic prosperity and her people. Profits from the slave trade led to the growth of major ports and cities and played an important part in turning Britain into a wealthy industrial country. The slave trade also provided employment for thousands of people and many individuals gained power and wealth.

Tropical crops
- The climate and land in the New World colonies were suited to the growing of luxury crops such as sugar, cotton, coffee and tobacco. Britain made large profits, particularly from the trade in sugar, which became very popular with British people.

Manufacturing
- Goods manufactured in Britain were used to buy enslaved Africans. These goods included textiles, metals such as iron, copper and brass, and metal goods such as pots, pans and cutlery.
- Cloth manufacturing grew, particularly in Manchester, due to supplies of slave-produced cotton.

Raw materials
- The slave trade was important in providing British industries with raw materials. The raw materials would be turned into manufactured goods in Britain and then sold for large profits in Europe.
- Liverpool grew wealthy from slave-grown cotton, while Bristol's wealth was partly based on slave-produced sugar.

Slaves cutting sugar cane

Industrial development

- Factories supplying goods to the slave traders developed.
- Banks and insurance companies that offered services to slave merchants expanded. London grew very wealthy as a result.
- Canals and railways were built as a result of investment of profits from the slave trade.
- Profits from the slave trade were invested in the development of industries.
- Some historians believe that the slave trade was central to Britain's industrial development. However, the slave trade was not always profitable. Changes in agriculture and advances in technology also contributed to Britain's wealth.

Wealth of ports and individuals

- Ports such as Bristol and Liverpool became wealthy trading centres due to their direct involvement in the trading of slaves. Liverpool became the main slave trading port.

- Other ports and cities profited from trading in goods connected with the slave trade.

- Huge fortunes were made by slave merchants, who often bought large country estates or built large town houses. Some merchants used their wealth from the slave trade to invest in banks, industries or new businesses.

Glasgow Gallery of Modern Art was built in 1780 as the townhouse of the wealthy tobacco lord, William Cunninghame of Lainshaw.

- Jobs such as shipbuilders, rope makers and dockworkers were created in British ports and many people gained employment in factories that supplied goods to the slave traders. Many British people owed their livelihood to the slave trade.

TOP TIP

'There is not a brick in the city but what is cemented with the blood of a slave.' Many buildings built for the slave trade can still be seen today.

Negative impact on the Caribbean

Negative impact of the slave trade on the Caribbean includes:

- Native populations such as the Arawak were cleared from the islands or killed by new diseases.
- The Caribbean became more volatile as slaves rebelled – St Domingue is a good example.
- The economy of the Caribbean came to rely on one crop – sugar – and plantations took out the diversity of smaller farms.
- Island landscapes were damaged and irreversibly changed by the growth of plantations.
- Slavery brought racism to the islands.

Quick Test

1. Name the two main British slave trading ports.
2. Which tropical crop made the most profit for Britain?
3. How did the slave trade benefit the Royal Navy?
4. How did merchants spend their fortunes made from the slave trade?

The Captive's experience and slave resistance

Living and working conditions on the plantations

Life on the plantations was arduous work for slaves. A plantation only grows one type of crop and on the British Caribbean islands the key crop was sugar. Most slaves would have been field hands or worked in the boiling houses. Their jobs involved:

- Working from sunrise to sunset. Breakfast was served only after a few hours of work in the morning.

- Slaves would work in the fields in 'gangs' – the first gang would be responsible for the heaviest work, the planting and cutting of the sugar cane. Children as young as 3-years-old would be put to work in the fields, tidying up leaves and sticks, and collecting food to feed animals.

- The sugar boiling house was dangerous work; sometimes slaves would be crushed in the sugar mills or burned by the sugar as it was heated to high temperatures to be refined into sugar crystals.

- Some slaves got to work in the 'Big House' – the plantation owner's house. They had longer hours, working 5 am until 10 pm and were responsible for the running of the house, cooking and cleaning.

Slaves lived together in huts on the plantations, some often resembling the huts in which they had lived in Africa. After sunset, slaves had some time to spend with their families. They would eat the food they had grown on their small patches of land, tell stories and sing songs. Marriage between slaves was encouraged – it would normally mean that babies would be born as a result and the plantation owner would acquire more slaves. If you were born into slavery you had no rights to freedom.

Slave masters often had relationships – willing or otherwise – with female slaves. Often this led to children being produced. The children who were born were mixed race or 'mulatto'. But as their mother was black, they were still considered slaves.

Slaves were not paid for the work they did. Sometimes a slave master might give small amounts of money as a reward for hard work achieved. Sometimes slaves would receive 'promotion' on the plantation to overseer, which meant the work was less hard and they were in charge of the other slaves.

Slaves were punished very cruelly to ensure they did not revolt and that the work was completed. They were subject to whippings, beatings, thumbscrews, shackles and isolation. Sometimes slaves would be sold to other plantations – this was traumatic, especially if families were split apart.

Other forms of slave labour on the Caribbean Islands

Some white men also worked as slave labour in the Caribbean, although they were 'indebted servants' rather than slaves in the way the black slaves were. This meant they normally owed huge debts and had chosen to work off their debts in the Caribbean by working on a plantation. They were not paid, or paid very little, for the work they completed. Working their way out of servitude could take years. However, it is not comparable with what happened to black slaves as they could achieve freedom and were not treated in the same way.

Resistance on the plantations

Resistance on the plantations was commonplace. Slaves never accepted their fate and would look for opportunities to resist slavery. This might be minor acts, like not working as hard as they could, destroying crops or acts of sabotage – destroying the wheels on carts so that sugar cane could not be transported. Slaves would run away, refuse to follow masters' instructions and spoil sugar in the boiling houses. These acts of resistance, if caught, carried very harsh punishments. To further humiliate the slaves, the masters rarely carried out the punishments themselves, they would get another slave to do it.

Fear of revolt

The system was designed to humiliate and degrade the slaves in the hope of stopping mass rebellions; masters were perfectly aware that they were outnumbered greatly by the number of slaves on the islands.

However, conversely, as time went on this is what happened. Factors that encouraged rebellions included:

- The continued cruel treatment of slaves – built-up resentment against masters.
- The French Revolution – showed the power of the people to overthrow their masters.
- The revolt on St Domingue – in 1791 enslaved Africans attacked plantation buildings with machetes and torches and killed white men and women, sending shockwaves around Europe. The rebellion was successful in setting up the first black colony – now known as Haiti.

In reaction to St Domingue, European slave owners just tried to punish their slaves even more harshly. But eventually the continued resistance fed into the idea of Abolition and the humanitarian concerns to end the trade.

Quick Test

1. What jobs did slaves do on the plantations?
2. What was an 'indebted servant'?
3. How did slaves resist their masters on the plantations?
4. What key rebellion sent shockwaves around Europe?

The abolitionist campaigns

The abolitionist movement

In 1787 the Society for the Abolition of the Slave Trade was formed in London. Its initial aim was to win over Members of Parliament to the abolitionist cause. **MP William Wilberforce** led the abolition campaign inside Parliament. He introduced bills to abolish the slave trade over a period of 18 years.

Arguments of the abolitionists

- Slave trade was un-Christian. It was immoral to use fellow human beings as slaves.
- Slave trade was inhumane. Slaves were denied their freedom and human rights.
- Slave trade was uneconomic. Britain's dependence on the slave trade hindered the development of domestic industries.

The abolitionists decided it was easier to campaign for the abolition of the slave trade than the abolition of slavery itself, since an important part of Britain's wealth depended on products produced by slaves and slave owners might demand compensation.

Abolitionist methods

Local and regional abolition committees were set up and organised meetings and activities including publishing pamphlets, posters and newspaper articles. Notable campaigners included:

- **Thomas Clarkson:** collected and publicised a wide range of evidence of the slave trade such as handcuffs, branding irons and thumbscrews; also, most importantly, the drawing of the Liverpool slave ship *The Brookes*.
- **Josiah Wedgwood:** china manufacturer who produced the society's slogan and design *'Am I Not A Man And A Brother?'* which appeared on cups, saucers and jewellery.
- **Olaudah Equiano:** gave first-hand evidence of his life as a slave. His book *An Interesting Life of Olaudah Equiano* was a best-seller and changed many people's views of the slave trade.
- **John Newton:** provided a first-hand account by a slaver. A former slave trade ship's captain who changed his opinion on slavery and became a clergyman; an influential preacher and writer on the cruelty of the slave trade.

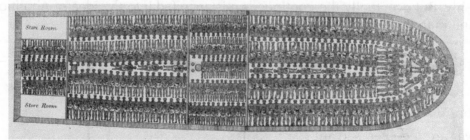

The drawing of the Liverpool slave ship The Brookes

Defenders of the trade

However, the slave trade had many important supporters.

- Plantation owners: the slave trade had made them very wealthy. Some bribed MPs to vote against abolition bills.
- There was a strong pro-slavery lobby within Parliament. Some MPs were also plantation owners or had businesses linked to the slave trade.
- The major ports of Liverpool and Bristol argued in favour of the slave trade.

The abolitionist campaign suffered a setback due to the French Revolution and Britain's war with France. The ideas of the abolitionists were regarded as being dangerous. It was much harder during this time for abolitionists to hold public meetings

The debate: why did the abolition campaign succeed?

In 1807 Parliament banned the slave trade. Why was the abolition campaign eventually successful?

- **Public opinion.** All levels of society were involved in the abolition campaign, reading abolitionist literature and attending meetings. Over 300 000 took part in the sugar boycott.
- **Pro-abolition MPs.** In 1792 the House of Commons voted in favour of the gradual abolition of the slave trade, although the bill was rejected by the House of Lords. Through these MPs' perseverance, an abolition bill was finally passed in Parliament in February 1807.
- **British economy.** Some historians argue that Britain's industries no longer depended on the triangular trade.
- **Slaves themselves.** At no point did slaves ever fully submit to slavery, they constantly fought against their masters and for their freedom. The importance of this should not be downplayed.

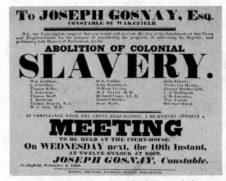

Petition calling for the abolition of slavery

TOP TIP

Has too much importance been given to William Wilberforce? It is important to remember the other key abolitionists who contributed. Many ordinary men and women also played important roles in the abolitionist campaigns.

Quick Test

1. Why did the abolitionists decide to concentrate on abolishing the slave trade rather than slavery?
2. What was the name of the former African slave who wrote a best-selling book about his experiences as a slave?
3. Name three groups who defended the slave trade.
4. Give three reasons for the success of the abolitionist campaign in 1807.

Timeline

- The Somerset Ruling. The law in England rules that a slave cannot be removed from Britain by force and sold into slavery.

- The Zong trial. The captain of the Zong is taken to court on charges of fraud against his insurance company after 132 slaves were murdered by being thrown overboard in order to claim insurance.

- The Society for the Abolition of the Slave Trade is formed.

- The Dolben Act introduces controls on the number of slaves ships can carry.

- The French Revolution (the revolutionaries opposed slavery). William Wilberforce introduces his first abolition bill, which is defeated.

- Over 300 000 people join the sugar boycott.

- 519 petitions against the slave trade, signed by 390 000 people are presented to Parliament.

- War with France. The abolition campaign suffers a decline in support.

- Foreign Slave Trade Act passed.

- Abolition of the Slave Trade Act. British Parliament bans the slave trade.

Biographies

Granville Sharp (1735–1813)

Granville Sharp was a civil servant and one of the founder members of the Society for the Abolition of the Slave Trade. He campaigned against the slave trade through the law courts. In 1772 he defended James Somerset and in 1783 he was involved in the court case against the captain of the Zong.

Hannah More (1745–1833)

Hannah More was a poet and author who supported the abolition of the slave trade. She helped organise the sugar boycott and encouraged other women to campaign against the slave trade.

James Stephen (1758–1832)

James Stephen joined the abolition movement after witnessing the treatment of slaves in the West Indies and played an influential role in the final stages of the abolition campaign. He used his background as a lawyer to draft a bill banning British subjects from participating in the slave trade with France and her allies. The bill passed and became the Foreign Slave Trade Act, which brought an end to two-thirds of Britain's slave trade.

William Wilberforce (1759–1833)

William Wilberforce was an MP for Hull and then for Yorkshire. He was introduced to the Society for the Abolition of the Slave Trade by his friend John Newton. He became the Society's leader and led the abolition campaign in Parliament. He was an inspirational speaker and debater who, despite facing strong opposition from supporters of the slave trade, introduced abolition bills every year from 1789 to 1807 and gradually won over Parliament to end the slave trade.

Olaudah Equiano (c.1745–1797)

Olaudah Equiano was enslaved as a child from what is now known as Nigeria and sold into slavery in the Caribbean. He wrote about his experiences in his book, *The Interesting Narrative of the Life of Olaudah Equiano*. He was sold to a Quaker merchant, Robert King who promised him he could buy his freedom for £40. King taught him to read and write and he was eventually able to purchase his freedom and came to live in London. He was instrumental in the Sons of Africa movement and his personal testimony and campaigning undoubtedly helped contribute to the Abolition of the Slave Trade.

Health and housing

In eighteenth and nineteenth century Britain, life expectancy was much lower than it is now. This was due to two very closely linked factors: poor health and poor housing.

Why was the health of the urban population so bad?

> **DID YOU KNOW?**
> The cholera epidemics actually improved living conditions in the long term, because they affected all classes of society. When the middle and upper classes were infected, the government was forced to act.

Lack of sanitation	• Open sewers attracted rats and flies and disease. • Communal toilets meant disease spread more easily. • Sewage from midden heaps and cesspools polluted the water supply.
Dirty water supply	• A shortage of fresh clean water meant disease spread quickly.
Lack of hygiene	• Few washing facilities meant people could not keep clean. • Clothes were difficult to wash, so lice were common. • Soap was expensive.
Poor diet	• A lack of fresh food in towns meant shortages of vitamins and minerals. • Alcoholism was common as people drank beer or gin because both tasted better than dirty water!
Killer diseases	• There was no cure for many diseases. • Thousands died every year of diseases such as cholera, tuberculosis, scarlet fever, smallpox, typhus and typhoid.
Poor housing	• Overcrowding meant diseases spread more easily. • Because of the window tax, people blocked up windows. This led to poor ventilation and air-borne diseases, for example influenza and tuberculosis. The tax was only removed in 1851.
Lack of support from the state	• The government took a laissez-faire approach, which meant no help for those in poverty that needed it.

Why did the situation improve?

Problem...	Tackled by...
Lack of sanitation	• **1848 Public Health Act** encouraged local councils to set up health boards to improve sanitation and water supply. • **1875 Public Health Act** forced local authorities to provide sewerage, drainage and clean water.
Dirty water supply	• Tackled by Health Acts above. • Reservoirs piped clean drinking water into cities.

Lack of hygiene	• The ending of the tax on soap/cheap carbolic soap meant people could wash properly. • Cotton clothes could be washed more easily and at higher temperatures.
Poor diet	• Improvements to farming meant there was a better food supply. • Better transport meant fresh meat, milk and vegetables could be bought in the cities. • Tea became a fashionable and healthy alternative to beer.
Killer diseases	• Greater medical knowledge and cleaner hospitals led to fewer deaths. • Better diet helped reduce deaths from tuberculosis. • Cholera and typhoid almost disappeared with cleaner water. • **1853 Vaccination Act** made smallpox vaccination compulsory.
Poor housing	• **1855 Nuisance Removal Act** allowed councils to demolish the worst slum housing. • **1875 Artisans' and Labourers' Dwellings Improvement Act** gave councils more power to demolish slums.
Lack of support from the state	• Still little help for the poorest families due to the laissez-faire attitude of government.

Why was the health of the urban population better than that of the rural population?

- Working hours were very long – exhaustion left people open to illness.
- Houses were damp – this led to the spread of diseases like tuberculosis.
- Diet lacked variety and vitamins.
- Living with animals often led to further diseases – bovine tuberculosis was common.

However, the health of the rural population was not as bad as the health of the urban population. Why was this?

- Less overcrowding, so diseases did not spread as quickly.
- Sanitation facilities were not shared with as many people.
- Water supply tended to be cleaner.
- Although the diet was poor it was generally better than in the towns and cities, with more fresh food available.

Quick Test

1. What were the killer diseases of the nineteenth century?
2. Why was the window tax bad for public health?
3. Which acts improved poor housing in the nineteenth century?
4. Why was health and housing better in the countryside?

Factories and mines

Coal mining

- Adult males tended to be 'hewers' who cut the coal with hand tools.
- Women and older children tended to be 'bearers', who carried coal up the mine shaft, or 'drawers', who pulled the coal in carts along the bottom of the mine to the shaft.
- Small children were often 'trappers' who opened and closed trap doors.

An investigation into mine conditions in 1840 revealed just how terrible they were. This encouraged the government to intervene.
New laws included:

- 1842: Children under 10 and all females banned from working in the mines.
- 1862: Single mine shafts declared illegal.
- 1872: Mine managers had to have certificates to prove that they were trained.

By 1900 mining was a safer job, but it was still hard, physical work in poor conditions.

Condition...	Tackled by...
Cutting coal	• In Scotland, the first coal cutting machinery ('Gartsherrie') used in 1864.
Poor ventilation: Lots of dust caused lung diseases like 'black spit'. It was also highly flammable.	• Two-shaft mines became more common. • Trap doors kept the air moving. • Ventilation fans installed from the 1860s onwards.
Transporting coal: Accidents occurred due to bearers falling and trappers being run over.	• From 1844, steam engines pulled hutches on rails. • Wire rope used from about 1850. • Steam-powered winding engines.
Flooding: Common as mines became deeper and drilled into underground lakes and rivers.	• Steam-powered pumps.
Gas: Some gases were explosive and others suffocated miners.	• Davy safety lamp invented in 1815. • Ventilation fans.
Roof falls: Very common before 1850. Miners were crushed to death or died of starvation if trapped.	• Wooden pit props were replaced by hydraulic, metal pit props by 1900.

Conditions in factories

- **Poor ventilation:** Lots of dust caused tuberculosis and other diseases.
- **Dangerous machinery:** Machines were unfenced and had to be cleaned or repaired while they were still running. No safety laws to protect workers.
- **Long working hours:** Before 1833, 14-hour days were common. Workers rarely had more than a 30-minute break. Tiredness caused many accidents.
- **Loud machinery:** The noise was literally deafening.
- **Hot, damp environment:** Factories were very humid in order to stop the cotton threads from breaking. This was very bad for the workers' health.
- **Risk of fire:** Due to the cotton fibres, explosions were common.

What was the impact of new technology?
- New machines like Arkwright's water frame and Crompton's mule sped up spinning and factories became more productive.
- Power looms increased the production of weaving.
- However, there was significant unemployment among hand spinners and weavers.
- New technology brought more accidents and more dust.
- Overall, the increased productivity meant that there were more jobs available.

Laws passed to improve conditions

1833 Factory Act	• No children under 9 allowed. • Maximum 8-hour working day for children aged 9–13. • Children were not allowed to clean machines while in motion.
1844 Factory Act	• Maximum 6½-hour working day for children under 13. • Maximum 12-hour working day for women and all under 18s. • Fencing of dangerous machinery became a legal requirement.
1847 Factory Act	• Maximum 10-hour working day for women and all under 18s.
1850 Factory Act	• Working day increased to 10½ hours.
1878 Factory Act	• No child under 10 was to be employed. • 10–14 year olds could only be employed for half days. • Women could work no more than 56 hours per week.

Despite these laws, by 1900 conditions in the factories were still dangerous and difficult.

Quick Test

1. What was 'black spit'?
2. Why was the Davy Safety Lamp important in improving miners' safety?
3. Why was repairing factory machinery so dangerous?
4. Name two pieces of technology that sped up factory work.

Canals and railways

Decline in the use of canals

By the 1830s Britain was connected by 4000 miles of canal networks. They were owned and maintained by different companies and had been built by navvies or 'navigators'. However, the invention of the steam engine put the canals into swift decline. They were slow, were affected by the weather and expensive in comparison to the trains.

Railways

The idea of putting a cart on a track was not new and wooden wagonways had been used before. By the early nineteenth century, improvements in iron production meant that metal tracks could be made and the invention of the steam locomotive in 1808 meant heavier loads could be pulled.

In 1825 the first public railway was opened between Stockton and Darlington. By the end of the nineteenth century almost every town and city in Britain was linked by a network of 22 000 miles of rail track.

How were the railways built?

Most of the railways were built by men who used picks, shovels, spades and barrows to shift the earth. Navvies built viaducts, cut into the sides of hills, blasted tunnels and built embankments and bridges.

Improvements to rail travel

Safety

- By the 1840s there was mechanical signalling on the tracks. Block signalling was introduced in 1889.
- By 1889 trains had continuous braking systems, which were enforced by the 1889 Regulation of Railways Act.

Comfort

- By the 1840s, third class carriages had seats and roofs. First and second class had toilets, heating and lighting from the 1870s.
- Journeys also became much quicker as the average speed rose. Building bridges also shortened journey times. The Tay Bridge and the Forth Bridge made travel in Scotland much quicker from the 1870s.

Forth Rail Bridge being built

What was the impact of the railway networks?

	Positive	Negative
Economy	• Investors in railways made fortunes. • Many jobs created by the railways. • Coal and iron industries boomed. • Shopping trips and other holidays boosted the economy in tourist towns.	• Towns not connected by train went into decline. • Canals declined. • Turnpike roads and coaching inns lost business.
Society	• Diet improved as fresh food could be brought in from the farms. • People could commute to work, meaning they did not have to live close to factories. • Postal service was more efficient.	• Some farmers had their land 'invaded' by noisy, dirty trains. • Fatal accidents when building the railways were common. • The Tay Bridge disaster (1879) killed 75 people due to faulty bridge design.

Quick Test

1. Why did canals go into decline?
2. What is a navvie?
3. How did railways help improve the economy?
4. How did railways help improve urban health?

Democratic reform up to 1867

Radical protest

The right to vote is key in a democratic country. In 1800 less than 3% of the population had the right to vote. People started to demand change and when this did not happen, some became more radical in their demands. In particular, the middle classes wanted to have more of a say – they felt they were generating wealth for the nation so it only seemed fair that they had a say in how things were run. The period 1815–1822 was known as Radicalism.

Peterloo Massacre

In 1815 the Corn Laws were passed, which raised the price of bread. This was very unpopular with the working classes but also the middle classes who claimed that trade and industry would suffer. The Radicals, led by Henry Hunt and William Cobbett, began to form an opposition. They organised meetings, marches and rallies:

- The Spa Field riot of 1816 was a largely peaceful protest and attempt to deliver a petition for electoral reform attended by 20 000 people. It turned troublesome when some breakaway protestors clashed with government troops.

- The Cato Street conspiracy of 1820 – a plot to blow up the Prime Minister and the cabinet and take over the country using force. However, an informant tipped off the police and the conspirators were either executed or transported to Australia.

- The Peterloo Massacre of 1819. On 16 August, Henry Hunt was speaking to around 80 000 people in St Peter's Field, Manchester. Local yeomanry attacked the crowd, killing 15 unarmed protesters and injuring hundreds of others.

These incidents of radical unrest showed that electoral change was required. The government only had to look at France to know that lack of change could bring about a revolution.

What did the 1832 Great Reform Act do?

- Gave the vote to 1 in 5 men, mostly in the middle classes.
- Gave more seats to the new industrial towns.
- Abolished rotten boroughs.

However, 90% of the population could not vote; the unelected House of Lords was very powerful; only wealthy, property-owning males could become MPs and the voting system was riddled with bribery and corruption.

The Chartists

Who?	• A group of campaigners based in the north of England.
How did they campaign?	• Held meetings. • Wrote letters and sent petitions to Parliament. • Published leaflets and newspapers. • Organised strikes and marches. • Would resort to violent demonstration if necessary.
Were they successful?	• They failed to gain support in Parliament or with the middle classes. • They raised awareness of the demand for reform. • Their influence can be seen in the 1867 Reform Act.

Universal male suffrage

Secret ballot voting system

Fairer distribution of seats/equal constituency size

Payment of MPs (and the removal of property qualifications)

Annual elections

The People's Charter

What did the 1867 Reform Act do?

For the first time, all male householders over 21 living in towns were given the vote. This meant some working class men were enfranchised for the first time and the electorate tripled.

There were still significant undemocratic features:

• No women could vote.
• Voting was public and open to bribery and corruption.
• Only wealthy people could become an MP.
• The House of Lords was very powerful.

Britain had some way to go to become a democracy.

What did the 1884 Act do?

The 1884 Act sought to further the effects of the 1867 Act. The counties were brought in line with the boroughs, and all men paying an annual rent of £10 or holding land valued at £10 were given the vote. It took the size of the British electorate to 5.5 million. In Scotland it gave 3 out of 5 men the vote and in England and Wales 2 out of 3 men had the vote.

Quick Test

1. How did the government deal with radical unrest?
2. Why were some people not satisfied with the 1832 Reform Act?
3. What did the Chartists want?
4. Why was the 1867 Reform Act seen as a step in the right direction?

Timeline

- – The Davy safety lamp invented.
- – The 'Peterloo Massacre'.
- – Stockton to Darlington railway opened.
- – The Great Reform Act passed.
- – Children under 10 banned from working in mines.
- – Window tax abolished.
- – Smallpox vaccinations made compulsory.
- – The Second Reform Act passed.
- – Forth Rail Bridge opens.

Biographies

Edward Jenner (1749–1823)

Jenner developed a vaccine against smallpox. He discovered that infecting people with the minor cowpox disease prevented them from getting smallpox. The word 'vaccine' comes from the Latin word *vacca* meaning cow. Smallpox was virtually wiped out in the 1970s and very few cases are diagnosed worldwide today.

Thomas Telford (1757–1834)

He was an engineer responsible for much of the transport infrastructure across Scotland and the rest of Britain. He designed and built canals, roads, harbours and tunnels. He built some of Britain's most impressive viaducts. Later in life he was known as the 'Colossus of Roads' due to his involvement with road building across Britain.

George Stephenson (1781–1848)

Stephenson was an engineer and inventor most famous for developing the 'Rocket' steam locomotive. The Rocket could travel at a record 36 miles per hour. Stephenson was responsible for building the Stockton to Darlington railway and designed the first passenger railway between Liverpool and Manchester.

Henry Hunt (1773–1835)

Henry Hunt was a radical speaker and huge influence on the Chartist movement. He was a superb public speaker and generated significant support for the radical movement for democracy. It was Henry Hunt who was speaking before the Peterloo massacre in 1819.

Benjamin Disraeli (1804–1881)

Disraeli was Conservative Prime Minister in the 1860s and 1870s. He played a key role as Chancellor of the Exchequer at the time of the 1867 Reform Act. He had significant rivalry with his Liberal counterpart, William Gladstone. Many credit Disraeli with creating a more modern Conservative Party. He also played a key role in Britain's involvement in the Suez Canal.

Divided society: poverty, housing, politics

In the late nineteenth and early twentieth centuries, there was little help available to the poor. It was commonly thought that poverty was caused by moral, personal or even genetic defects. Politicians believed in *laissez-faire*, that is, they thought it was not the responsibility of the government to interfere in people's private lives.

What help was available to the poor?

The Poor Law

The Poor Law, passed in 1834, created work houses (or poor houses in Scotland) to provide help for the needy. The conditions were deliberately harsh so that it would be a last resort. Families were split up, inmates were forced to wear a uniform and the diet was poor. One Victorian writer referred to poor houses as 'prisons for the poor'. They were feared and hated, so only about 10% of people who needed relief actually received it.

Dinner time at St Pancras Workhouse in London, circa 1911

Self help

In 1850 a Scotsman called Samuel Smiles wrote the book *Self-Help*. Smiles wrote that the best way to get out of poverty was through hard work and effort. He wrote 'God helps those who help themselves.' Unfortunately, Smiles failed to recognise that poverty was often caused by factors outwith an individual's control. Smiles' book reinforced the idea that if you were poor it was your own fault.

Charity

Many charitable organisations were formed at the turn of the century to help the poor. The Salvation Army, Dr Barnado's and the YMCA were all formed during this period. While they did help the poor, they were uncoordinated and many poor people received no effective help.

Slum housing in Glasgow, 1861

Why did attitudes towards poverty change?

Investigations into poverty

Towards the end of the nineteenth century, several writers studied the lives of the poor. Charles Booth wrote *Life and Labour of the People in London* between 1886 and 1903 and Seebohm Rowntree wrote *Poverty: A Study of Town Life* in 1901 about the city of York.

What did the investigations discover?

- Rowntree calculated that £1·08 a week was the minimum income to keep a family above the 'poverty line'. Anyone living below this was deemed to be in poverty.
- According to their calculations 30% of the population were living below the poverty line.
- They identified the causes of poverty as sickness, old age, unemployment, low wages and large families rather than laziness and moral failings as had been previously thought.

The reports were influential because they used statistical data that proved that poverty was a major problem in Britain.

Emergence of the Labour Party

The emergence of the Labour Party after 1900 gave the working class a party to represent their interests. Both the Liberals and the Conservatives had to compete with Labour for working class votes, so were forced to take the issue of poverty seriously.

National security

The Boer War of 1889–1902 revealed that almost 25% of volunteers for the army were rejected on grounds of ill health. This figure was even higher in cities. The government was concerned that Britain could not protect its Empire or win a war if its young men were not fit enough to fight because of childhood poverty.

Genuine concern

A new generation of politicians were genuinely concerned about poverty. The Liberal Leader David Lloyd George had been brought up in a poor family in Wales.

Quick Test

1. What does *'laissez-faire'* mean?
2. Why was the help available to the poor ineffective?
3. What was the poverty line?
4. What did investigations of Booth and Rowntree reveal as the main causes of poverty?

Liberal Reforms 1906–1914

The reforms

Between 1906 and 1914 the Liberal government introduced a series of social reforms to improve the lives of the poor. Five main groups in society were targeted.

The young

There was genuine concern that Britain would lose its position as a global power in the future due to the poor health of children. Three reforms were passed.

- **Education (Provision of Meals) Act 1906**
  - Local councils could raise taxes to **pay f**or free school meals for children.
  - It was not compulsory, however, so many councils did nothing and the problem was not solved.
- **Education (Administrative Provisions) Act 1907**
  - Every child would receive three free medical inspections during their school career.
  - This was successful in identifying chronic health problems, but did nothing to treat them.
- **Children's Charter 1908**
  - Children were banned from begging, smoking and drinking alcohol.
  - Special children's courts and prisons were introduced to keep juveniles away from adult criminals.

Children drinking and smoking, circa 1905

The old

David Lloyd George famously said that the elderly who had worked all of their lives should not be allowed to reach 'the gates of the tomb … through the brambles and thorns of poverty'.

- **Old Age Pensions Act 1908**
  - Entitled people over 70 who earned between £21 and £31 a year to a maximum weekly pension of 25 pence.
  - This was 10 pence less than the amount needed to stay above the poverty line.
  - Life expectancy for the working poor was much less than 70 so most people died before receiving a pension.

The sick

The poor often struggled to pay for medical treatment. There was no free healthcare so illness often went untreated, leading to absence from work.

- **National Insurance Act (Part 1) 1911**
  - A contributory scheme in which the worker paid 4 pence, the employer 3 pence and the government 2 pence a week.
  - If a worker was absent through ill health they would receive benefits for 26 weeks.
  - Critics argue that the contributions to the scheme from workers' wages meant they were paid less, so actually made poverty worse.

THINK POINT

The turn of the century was a very unsettled time in Britain. The campaign for women's suffrage, European conflict in the build-up to the First World War and political problems in Ireland were all major problems for the government. Given this context, should the Liberal reforms be considered a success or a failure?

The unemployed

Reforms were introduced to help those out of work.

- **Labour exchanges**
  - The government introduced labour exchanges where workers could register their skills and employers would advertise their vacancies. By 1914, 3000 people were finding employment every day.
  - Critics argue that the exchanges only helped people find other low paid and temporary work, so did not improve poverty.
- **National Insurance Act (Part 2) 1911**
  - A contributory scheme that covered workers in specific heavy industries if they became unemployed.
  - It was limited because it only covered around two million workers.
  - Contributions from wages made poverty worse.

The employed

The Liberals also introduced a series of reforms to tackle the issue of low pay and poor working conditions, for example:

- The Coal Mines Act (1908) introduced an 8-hour working day for miners.
- The Minimum Wage Act (1912) set up a minimum wage for miners.

How successful were the Liberal reforms?

Some argue that while the reforms did go some way to easing the problems of poverty, they did not solve them. Many people were still living below the poverty line defined by Rowntree.

However, others argue that the Liberal reforms were crucial in ending the 'laissez-faire' attitude towards poverty. For the first time ever the government introduced laws to improve the living standards of the people. The reforms have been described as 'the greatest ever passed by one government up to that time'.

Quick Test

1. Which five groups did the Liberals focus their reforms upon?
2. Why were the Liberals concerned about the health of children?
3. Why can it be argued that some of the reforms actually made the problems of poverty worse?
4. Why can it be argued that the reforms were successful, even though they did not eradicate poverty?

Social impact of the Second World War in Britain

The interwar years

Despite the best efforts of the Liberal government between 1906 and 1914, there was still a significant problem of poverty in Britain between the First and Second World Wars. These problems were made worse by a global depression triggered by the Wall Street Crash, declining industry and high levels of unemployment. The outbreak of the Second World War and the formation of the wartime coalition government brought the issue of poverty into the limelight once more.

The effects of the Second World War on attitudes to poverty

Bombing

The German Air Force targeted big industrial cities in Britain. Both rich and poor were affected. Over 61 000 civilians lost their lives and over four million homes were damaged or destroyed. Even Buckingham Palace was bombed. Wealthy people were now forced to rely on government help and rich and poor found themselves shoulder to shoulder in air raid shelters. Support increased for government intervention into social problems.

Effects of bombing in Aberdeen

Rationing

Rationing was introduced to ensure that there was a fair distribution of food and fuel for all people. Rich and poor were equally affected and this equality of sacrifice brought about a change in social attitudes.

Evacuation

Children from inner city areas were evacuated to rural areas to protect them from bombing raids. People in the country were often horrified at the poverty they witnessed among the children they homed. They gained a much better understanding of the problems of urban poverty and demanded something was done.

The Beveridge Report and the Five Giants

In 1942 the coalition government asked Sir William Beveridge to produce a report to show how a welfare state could be created. Sir William Beveridge had been a key adviser to the Liberals when they passed their social reforms between 1906 and 1914. A welfare state is one that looks after its people 'from the cradle to the grave', i.e. from birth to death.

He identified major problems, which he called 'the Five Giants' of poverty. He argued that all five needed to be eradicated if Britain was to lift all of its citizens out of poverty and hardship.

These were:

- **Want** – A lack of money
- **Disease** – Illness and poor health
- **Squalor** – Poor quality housing
- **Ignorance** – Lack of education
- **Idleness** – Unemployment

In order to tackle these giants, Beveridge recommended a social security system that would be:

Comprehensive	It would cover all problems relating to poverty, from birth to death.
Universal	It would be available to everyone.
Contributory	People would make weekly payments to the scheme through their wages.
Non-means-tested	Benefits would be available to all, regardless of ability to pay.
Compulsory	All workers would have to contribute.

Inter-war reforms

It is important to realise that not all social reforms of this time were passed by the post-war Labour government. The 1944 Education Act for example was passed during the wartime coalition government by the Tory MP R.A. Butler. It set a minimum leaving age, which meant that all pupils had to stay at school until the age of 15.

DID YOU KNOW?

Before the Beveridge Report and his recommendations to improve the health of the nation, a common present when someone reached 21 was to pay to have all of their teeth removed and false ones put in their place. This was because dental hygiene was so bad!

Quick Test

1. How did the Second World War change attitudes to poverty?
2. What is a welfare state?
3. What were the 'Five Giants' of poverty?
4. In order to effectively tackle the giants of poverty, what did Beveridge recommend a social security system should be?

Labour reforms – the welfare state, 1945–1951

At the end of the Second World War, Labour won a landslide election and the new Prime Minister, Clement Attlee, planned to create a welfare state that would tackle all 'Five Giants'.

- **Want** – A lack of money.
- **Disease** – Illness and poor health.
- **Squalor** – Poor quality housing.
- **Ignorance** – Lack of education.
- **Idleness** – Unemployment.

1945 Labour election poster

Social security

To tackle Want, the Labour government passed three acts;

- **National Insurance (Industrial Injuries) Act 1946**
  In return for weekly contributions, the government would provide benefits for anyone injured in the workplace who could not consequently earn a wage.

- **National Insurance Act 1946**
  A contributory scheme that entitled workers to unemployment, sickness, maternity and widows' benefits, a retirement pension and a funeral grant. The aim was to provide insurance 'from the cradle to the grave'.

- **National Assistance Act 1948**
  The previous reforms were only for people in work, but the government wanted to create a 'safety net' for those who could not afford to contribute to National Insurance. People could apply for further benefits if National Insurance did not cover their needs.

Criticisms of National Insurance

- Due to rising prices and wages after the war, welfare benefits in 1948 were only 19% of the average wage, not enough to lift people out of poverty.
- Too many people were therefore forced to apply for national assistance.

Health

To tackle Disease, Labour created the National Health Service (NHS), in 1948. It was set up with three main principles: it should be universal, comprehensive and free at the point of use. This meant it would be available to everybody, would cover any medical problem and would be funded by taxation, not by charges for treatment.

In the first year of the NHS, millions benefited from free glasses, prescriptions and dental care. The biggest criticism was its cost. By 1950 the NHS was costing £358 million a year and taxes only paid for a fifth of this. In 1951 the government was forced to abandon

the principle of 'free at the point of use' and introduce charges for false teeth and glasses.

Despite this, the NHS has been described as 'the single greatest achievement of the welfare state'.

TOP TIP

Make a timeline of the social reforms in this topic. Colour code it to show which reforms were passed by the Liberals, wartime coalition government or Labour. This will help you to understand the chronology of social reform in Britain.

Housing reform

Overcrowding and slums had been a problem before the war and this was worsened by the destruction of approximately 700 000 homes in bombing raids.

Despite a shortage of building materials and labour force, the government built 200 000 homes a year between 1945 and 1951. Even this was not adequate, however, as the post-war baby boom years saw a rapid increase in population and demand for housing. A 1951 census showed that there were 750 000 fewer houses than were required.

Education reform

The Labour government at first inherited the 1944 Education Act or 'Butler Act', which aimed to provide free secondary education for all and establish 3 different categories of schools – Grammar, Secondary Modern and Technical. However, there were immediate problems facing these proposals – a shortage of decent buildings available for the new schooling plans meant that Attlee had to focus on building new primary schools rather than implementing the tripartite system. Thus, few technical schools were actually built. Also introduced was the divisive 11+ exam, which determined if a student went to a Grammar or Secondary Modern. In 1946, Comprehensive schooling became Labour policy.

Was the Labour government successful in creating a welfare state?

Some historians have criticised the reforms, arguing that poverty was not eradicated as outlined by William Beveridge.

Others have a much more positive view of the Labour government's achievements. Given that Britain was nearly bankrupted by the Second World War, they argue that Labour introduced a set of long-lasting reforms that promoted a fair society. While poverty was not eradicated, help was provided to those in need and the general living standard of the poor was raised.

Quick Test

1. Which acts did Labour pass to solve the problem of Want?
2. Why can it be argued that Labour's social security reforms were ineffective?
3. What was the biggest criticism of the NHS?
4. Why did demand for housing grow after the war?

Timeline

- Seebohm Rowntree begins investigating urban poverty in London.

- Formation of the Labour Party.

- The Liberals win a landslide election victory and begin introducing social reforms to improve the lives of the poor.

- Outbreak of the First World War.

- The Wall Street Crash in America triggers a global depression, which leads to a decline in British industry and increased unemployment.

- Outbreak of the Second World War leads to the suspension of party politics and the creation of the wartime coalition government.

- The Beveridge Report is published.

- Elections held at the end of the war lead to a landslide victory for the Labour Party.

- The creation of the NHS.

Biographies

Charles Booth (1840–1916)

Booth was born into a wealthy family of shipbuilders and merchants in Liverpool. He was sceptical about a claim made by a politician that 25% of the population of London lived in poverty and so decided to investigate. He discovered that the figure was actually closer to 35%. His investigations, based on statistical data, proved to be very influential among politicians.

Seebohm Rowntree (1871–1954)

Born into the wealthy sweet manufacturing family, Rowntree was influenced by Booth and decided to investigate poverty in York. He discovered that almost 30% of the population were living in poverty. He defined the 'poverty line', stating the minimum amount of money needed to afford the basic necessities of life.

David Lloyd George (1863–1945)

Lloyd George was Chancellor at the time of the Liberal Reforms. He was responsible for the 'People's Budget' of 1909, which increased taxes on land to pay for welfare reforms. He was instrumental in setting up old age pensions and also in introducing sickness benefits.

William Beveridge (1879–1963)

Beveridge was a social reformer who advised the Liberal government on their welfare reforms. The wartime coalition government during the Second World War asked him to write a report recommending how a welfare state could be created. His report identified the 'Five Giants' of poverty and was widely supported by the British people.

Clement Attlee (1883–1967)

Attlee was the leader of the Labour Party during the Second World War and acted as the Deputy Prime Minister to Winston Churchill in the wartime coalition government. In 1945 he campaigned in elections by promising to implement the recommendations of the Beveridge Report. His party won a landslide victory and he set about introducing welfare reforms.

Imperial Russia – government and people

In 1894, Nicholas Romanov II became Tsar of Russia. He was a weak and poor leader, more interested in spending time with his family than ruling the country. Russia was an autocracy, which meant that the Tsar had absolute power over his subjects. Despite this, Russia was a very difficult country to govern.

Why was Russia difficult to govern?

Size
- The Russian Empire was huge. It contained approximately one seventh of all of the land on Earth.

DID YOU KNOW?
The only way to get from the west to the east of Russia was via the Trans-Siberian railway. This took a week!

Environment
- Russia was a cold, inhospitable place to live.
- Only a small part of the land was suitable for farming; most of the land was made up of frozen tundra, dense forest and desert.

People
- The Russian Empire contained over 130 million people, but less than half were ethnically Russian.
- Many people could not speak the Russian language and belonged to religions other than the official Orthodox Russian Church.
- The Tsarist government introduced the policy of Russification. Ethnic groups were banned from speaking their local language and were forced to learn Russian. They felt that their different ways of life were under attack.

Russian society

Peasants
- In 1914, peasants made up 85% of the population. The vast majority of these were poor, uneducated and illiterate. Their life expectancy was less than 40 years.
- Agricultural methods were backward and inefficient. Their way of farming (strip farming) was back breaking and led to low yields. They had little modern technology and used hand-made tools to work the land.

Workers
- In the cities, poor industrial workers endured terrible conditions.
- Heavy industries such as steel, coal and iron were growing fast. Despite this, wages remained low and conditions were very poor. Accidents in the workplace led to many deaths.

- Workers were forced to work overtime, sometimes up to 16 hours a day. They lived in overcrowded barracks provided by factory owners. These lacked basic sanitation.
- Occasionally workers would strike, but they were defeated by violence and bloodshed.

Middle class
- The Russian middle class grew at the start of the twentieth century due to the growth of business and industry. They were mainly wealthy and supportive of the Tsar as they owed their wealth to the government.

Nobles
- The super wealthy aristocracy owned over a quarter of the land, despite making up less than 1% of the population. They owned fabulous palaces, wore ostentatious fashions and dined at expensive restaurants.

Russian noblewoman, circa 1895

How did the Tsar rule Russia?

The Tsar was an autocrat, that is, he had ultimate authority in government. He could not rule such a vast country on his own, however, so there was a system of government to help keep control.

Church	• The Church taught the Russian people that the Tsar was the 'Little Father', a living God.
Ministers	• The Tsar appointed ministers to run the government. They reported to him and he made the final decisions. He had the power to dismiss them whenever he saw fit.
Okhrana	• A secret police force whose function was to spy on potential enemies. • Suspected dissidents could be tortured, executed or exiled to the frozen wastes of Siberia.
Cossacks	• The Cossacks were violent horse-backed warriors who were used to put down any strikes or protests against the Tsar.
Russification	• A policy that enforced Russian as the only official language. • Ensured Russian was the only language used in education and in the legal system. • The Russian Orthodox Church was the only recognised religion.

Quick Test

1. What does autocracy mean?
2. What was the policy of Russification?
3. What problems did the workers and peasants face in Tsarist Russia?
4. How did the Tsar keep control of Russia?

1905 Revolution – causes and events

Opposition to the Tsar

Several groups were prepared to oppose the Tsar.

- **Kadets** or **Liberals**: Middle class professionals who supported the Tsar but opposed autocracy. They wanted a democracy in which the Tsar would share power with a freely elected Parliament.
- **Socialist Revolutionaries:** Also known as the Peasants' Party, believed that all land should be confiscated and given to the peasants. They wanted to overthrow the Tsar.
- **Socialist Democrats**: Followed the teachings of Karl Marx; aimed to overthrow the Tsar and create a socialist state in which all land and wealth would be shared equally.

In 1903 the Socialist Democrats split into two groups: Bolsheviks and Mensheviks.

Bolsheviks	Mensheviks
<ul><li>Led by Lenin.</li><li>Wanted a workers' revolution with no middle class involvement.</li><li>Believed revolution should be led by trained 'professional revolutionaries'.</li><li>Prepared to use violence if necessary.</li></ul>	<ul><li>Led by Julius Martov.</li><li>Wanted a workers' revolution but with the help of the middle class.</li><li>Did not believe in use of violence.</li></ul>

TOP TIP

In order to fully understand the political ideas of the Bolsheviks, you should research the beliefs of Karl Marx as set out in 'The Communist Manifesto'.

The 1905 Revolution

In 1905 resentment among the workers and peasants grew and protests against the Tsar's government began.

What caused the 1905 Revolution?

- **Economic problems**: Peasants were taxed heavily to pay for improvements in industry. Poor harvests led to starvation.
- **The Russo-Japanese War:** Russia and Japan went to war over Manchuria. Russia's defeat led to protests about the incompetence of the Tsar.
- **Bloody Sunday:** In January 1905 a priest, Father Gapon, organised a peaceful march of 200 000 on the Winter Palace. The Tsar ordered the Cossacks to attack and a massacre occurred.

1905 Revolution: key events

- Landowners' homes were burned and looted.
- The Tsar's uncle was assassinated.
- The middle classes joined the protests.
- Sailors in the war rebelled against the Tsar.

- In September the Tsar signed a peace treaty with Japan.
- In October a general strike spread throughout major industrial cities.
- In December the Tsar used troops returning from the war to stop demonstrations.
- The revolution ended and the Tsar survived.

Fire in Odessa after the mutiny aboard the Potemkin battleship

What changed after 1905?

In October 1905 the Tsar signed the October Manifesto. He promised:
- A Duma (Parliament) elected by the people
- Civil rights
- Uncensored newspapers and the right to form political parties.

However, the Tsar did not give in to demands for greater democracy. The Duma had very little power and was inherently weak because the Tsar could dissolve it whenever he liked. While free speech had been guaranteed in 1905, censorship of newspapers continued.

Stolypin's reforms

In order to regain control the Tsar appointed a new Prime Minister, Peter Stolypin. He was known for his brutal punishment of revolutionaries, but he also introduced reforms to tackle some of the problems of poverty.

Countryside	Peasants were encouraged to buy land to create larger fields, yielding greater harvests. While production of food did increase slightly, there was not enough land to go round and farming methods remained backward.
Cities	Stolypin wanted to improve Russian industry. From 1906–14 there was an industrial boom in Russia. However, very few improvements were made to working and living conditions and as more workers moved into the cities, living conditions actually worsened.

Quick Test

1. Which groups opposed the Tsar?
2. What were the main causes of the 1905 Revolution?
3. Why was the Duma weak?
4. Who was appointed Prime Minister after 1905 and what did he do?

February Revolution – causes, events and effects

Causes of the 1917 February Revolution

War at the Front
- The Russian army suffered terrible casualties in the First World War. By the end of 1917 **1.3 million** soldiers had been killed, **4.2 million** had been wounded and **2.417 million** taken prisoner.
- Russian soldiers blamed the Tsarist regime for the military defeats.

War at home
- The war caused huge economic problems for ordinary Russians.
- Agricultural output fell as millions of peasants and farm workers were conscripted into the army.
- Almost all of the trains were commandeered to take supplies to the front. This caused food and fuel shortages in the cities.
- Food and fuel prices increased but wages decreased. This led to strikes.

Influence of Rasputin
- The Tsar's son and heir, Alexis, suffered from the blood disease haemophilia. This was kept secret from the people.
- In desperation the Tsar sought help from a holy man called Rasputin. He was a coarse and drunken peasant, but was rumoured to have healing powers.
- He became part of the Tsar's entourage and eventually one of his most trusted advisers. He even influenced government decisions.
- The nobles were outraged and questioned the Tsar's judgement.

Unpopularity of the Tsarina
- In 1915 the Tsar went to the front to take command of the army. He left his German wife Alexandra to run the government.
- Rumours spread that Alexandra was a German spy.
- She was rumoured to be having an affair with Rasputin. This is probably untrue, but it increased the unpopularity of the royal family.

The Tsarina and her son, Alexis

The events of the February Revolution

- On 14 February 40 000 workers from the Putilov engineering works went on strike demanding higher wages and an end to food and fuel shortages.

- On International Women's Day (19 February) and the days that followed, over 200 000 workers took to the streets of Petrograd demanding cheaper food, higher wages and a new government.

- 27 February was the turning point. The Petrograd Garrison, which had been ordered to fire upon the protestors, mutinied and joined the revolution.

- The Tsar tried to return to Petrograd by train but was stopped by revolutionary rail workers.

- On 2 March the Tsar abdicated.

The February Revolution

The aftermath of the February Revolution

The abdication left a power vacuum that was filled by an alliance between the Provisional Government and the Petrograd Soviet, known as **Dual Power.**

- **Provisional Government:** Made up of ex-members of the Duma. They decided that they did not have the authority to make major decisions because they were not democratically elected. This was a fatal weakness. Russia needed strong leadership, but the Provisional Government did not provide it.

- **Petrograd Soviet:** A council of soldiers and sailors. They issued 'Order Number One', a proclamation that effectively gave them control of the army, railways and postal services. The Minister of War wrote: 'the Provisional Government exists only while this is permitted by the Soviet'.

In the early months of Dual Power, the Provisional Government did introduce some reforms, mainly aimed at increasing civil rights. These reforms did little to solve the main problems facing Russia: the continuing disaster of the war, the food and fuel shortages in the cities and the issue of land reform.

THINK POINT

It is sometimes said that the Provisional Government was doomed to failure from the start. Do you agree with this statement? What evidence would you use to explain your answer?

Quick Test

1. Why was the First World War so unpopular in Russia?
2. How did Rasputin damage the reputation of the Royal Family?
3. Why was the Petrograd Soviet more powerful than the Provisional Government?
4. Why did the Provisional Government fail to provide strong leadership?

October Revolution – causes, events, effects

The October Revolution

Events leading to the October Revolution

- **March 1917:** Lenin returned from exile in Switzerland and immediately argued for a second revolution. He issued a document known as the **'April Theses'**. This was simplified into two slogans; **'Peace, bread and land'** and **'All power to the Soviets'**. Bolsheviks were the only party to promise an end to the war.
- **July 1917 (July Days):** Bolsheviks attempted to lead a second revolution against the Provisional Government. They were defeated and Lenin fled to Finland.
- **August 1917:** General Kornilov threatened to invade Petrograd. The leader of the Provisional Government, Aleksandr Kerensky, asked the Bolshevik Red Guard to protect the city. They were given machine guns and rifles.
- Although Kornilov never reached Petrograd, the Bolsheviks were seen as saviours and kept their weapons. Kerensky and the Provisional Government looked weak and incompetent.

Lenin was convinced that conditions were perfect for a second revolution. He returned from exile in Finland and convinced the other Bolsheviks, who eventually agreed. Trotsky was put in charge of planning the revolution.

> **TOP TIP**
>
> When the Bolsheviks took power in October 1917 they changed the Russian calendar to make it match the western world. Because of this you will sometimes see the February Revolution referred to as the March Revolution and the October Revolution as the November Revolution.

Key events of the October Revolution

- On 24 October the Bolshevik Red Guards occupied railway stations, telephone exchanges, power stations and took control of the bridges over Petrograd's many canals and rivers.
- On 25 October Red Guards surrounded the Winter Palace, which contained the remnants of the Provisional Government. At 9pm the battleship Aurora, crewed by revolutionary sailors, opened fire on the Winter Palace. The defenders of the palace fled and a small group of Bolsheviks entered and confronted the Provisional Government, who officially surrendered.
- Bolsheviks took control of Petrograd.

The Soviets in power

- In December 1917 Lenin set up the Chekha to suppress opponents of the Bolsheviks. Tens of thousands of civilians were executed without trial between 1918 and 1921 – this became known as the Red Terror.
- In March 1918 Lenin withdrew Russia from the War (Treaty of Brest-Litovsk).

Why did the Reds win the Civil War, 1918–21?

The Reds (Bolsheviks)	The Whites (Anti-Bolsheviks)
• Controlled the industrialised areas and most of the railways; could transport soldiers and supplies quickly.	• Were scattered around Russia and found it difficult to communicate or transport troops.
• An effective and disciplined fighting force.	• Uncoordinated and ill disciplined.
• Depicted themselves as patriots fighting in defence of Russia; claimed the Whites were controlled by foreign enemies.	• Had help from Britain, France and the USA. However, they did not send enough troops or supplies to make a difference.
• Were well fed and supplied. Lenin introduced 'War Communism'. He requisitioned grain from peasants and took control of factories.	• Were poorly supplied.

Nature of the Soviet state

The economy

War communism caused a mass famine that killed 5 million people. Lenin was therefore forced to introduce the New Economic Policy (NEP) which:

- Stopped grain requisitioning.
- Maintained state control over major industries such as coal, oil, steel and railways. Smaller industries were allowed to be run under private ownership.
- Introduced a new currency and allowed the buying and selling of goods.
- Successfully ended famine in the countryside.

Despite this, many Bolsheviks saw it as a betrayal of communist ideology.

Other changes

The Communists improved standards of literacy, increased women's rights and invested in the arts. However, poverty had barely improved; the people had endured a crippling famine, they lived in fear of the Chekha and they still could not vote.

Quick Test

1. Why was Lenin's return to Russia in March 1917 significant?
2. How did the Kornilov revolt help the Bolsheviks?
3. What promise did Lenin keep when the Bolsheviks took power?
4. Why was Trotsky an important figure for the Bolsheviks?

Timeline

1894 – Tsar Nicholas II becomes Tsar of Russia.

1905 – Russia breaks out in open revolt against the Tsar.

December 1905 – The Tsar regains control of Russia by deploying troops returning from the Russo-Japanese War.

1914 – Russia joins the war on the side of the Triple Entente.

1915 – The Tsar takes control of the Russian army, leaving the Tsarina in charge of the government.

February 1917 – Russia breaks out in revolution, the Tsar abdicates and the Provisional Government and the Petrograd Soviet rule with Dual Power.

October 1917 – The Bolsheviks lead a revolution against the Provisional Government, who eventually surrender and leave the Bolsheviks in charge.

March 1918 – Lenin signs the Treaty of Brest-Litovsk and pulls Russia out of the First World War.

1918–1921 – Russia erupts into Civil War between the Bolshevik Reds and the anti-Bolshevik Whites. In 1921 the Reds win.

Biographies

Tsar Nicholas Romanov II (1868–1918)

A member of the Romanov royal family, Nicholas ruled Russia from 1894 until 1917. He did little to solve the social problems in Russia and so peasants and workers became increasingly dissatisfied with his leadership. He survived an attempted revolution in 1905, but was forced to abdicate after the February Revolution in 1917.

Grigory Rasputin (1869–1916)

Rasputin was a peasant holy man who was rumoured to have supernatural healing powers. He was very unpopular among the Russian nobility because he was seen as a coarse and drunken peasant. His relationship with the Tsar was a contributing factor to the outbreak of the February Revolution.

Aleksandr Kerensky (1881–1970)

Kerensky was an important political figure after the February Revolution as he was the only man who was a member of the Provisional Government and the Petrograd Soviet. He was the Minister for War during the July Days and later became Prime Minister.

Lenin (1870–1924)

Lenin was the leader of the Bolsheviks and a professional revolutionary. He was in exile during the February Revolution, but immediately called for a second revolution on his return. After the October Revolution he became the leader of Russia. He ruled as a dictator and his policies were crucial in keeping the Red Army supplied during the Civil War.

Leon Trotsky (1879–1940)

Trotsky was Lenin's number two in the Bolsheviks. He was elected as Chairman of the Petrograd Soviet prior to the October Revolution. He planned the revolution in minute detail and was also in charge of the Red Army during the Civil War. He ensured discipline and made sure that the Red Army was an effective fighting force.

Weimar Germany

What happened at the end of World War I?

- German sailors mutinied at Kiel and Wilhelmshaven naval bases. The British blockade of Germany's ports meant food was not getting through and Germans were starving. The allies refused to sign a cease-fire unless the Kaiser abdicated.
- The Kaiser abdicated on 10 November 1918. The next day the cease-fire was signed and the First World War ended with Germany's defeat.
- The Weimar Republic was formed.

The Treaty of Versailles

There was widespread hatred among Germans of the terms of the Treaty of Versailles.

Term	Impact
Diktat	Resented being forced to sign the Treaty without negotiation.
War Guilt Clause	Hated being blamed for something that was not solely their fault.
Reparations of £6.6 billion	Starvation continued after the war; loss of industrial land hindered recovery.
Severe reductions to army and navy. No air force allowed.	Humiliating, left Germany vulnerable to attack. Anger that no other country was treated similarly.
Excluded from League of Nations.	Insulted, isolated from future negotiations.

As a result, Germans called those who signed the Treaty 'November criminals'. These politicians formed the new Weimar government.

The Weimar government

A new government was formed in Weimar with a set of rules called a constitution. The first President was Friedrich Ebert. The constitution created the Reich (state) as a democratic country with a Chancellor and the Reichstag (parliament). Elections took place every four years and every German over the age of 20 could vote.

A President (voted for every seven years) had the power to prevent laws from being passed and they could close the Parliament in the event of a 'national emergency' (Article 48).

What were the problems for the new Weimar government?
- Association with signing the very unpopular Treaty of Versailles.
- Rebuilding Germany after the war was difficult.
- Many wanted the return of a monarchy.
- Some thought the new republic was too left wing.

There were several attempts to overthrow the Weimar government. There was a left-wing revolt in 1919 (Spartacist Revolt) and two right-wing revolts: the Kapp Putsch in 1920 and the Munich Putsch in 1923.

TOP TIP

Putsch = German word for uprising
Mutiny = A revolt by soldiers or sailors
Abdicate = When a monarch gives up the throne
Reichstag = German parliament

Munich Beerhall Putsch

When?	November 1923
Where?	Munich, Bavaria
Who?	Right-wing/Nazi group led by Hitler
Why?	To overthrow the government and start a Nationalist revolution.
What?	• 600 armed followers stormed a meeting of Bavarian politicians. Hitler forced those politicians to support him. • 3000 Nazis marched the next day and were met with armed police. 16 Nazis were killed and Hitler was arrested. • Hitler was put on trial for treason and sent to Landsberg Castle jail. • The trial gave Hitler publicity and he became nationally known. • Hitler used his time in prison to write *Mein Kampf*.

Economic crises

In response to the crisis in the Ruhr and other economic problems, the Weimar government decided to print more money in order to keep paying wages. Businesses put up prices. This resulted in *hyperinflation* – prices rose faster than people could spend the money.

163	250	463	1465	3465	69 000	1 512 000	1 743 000 000	201 000 000 000
Dec 1922	Jan 1923	Mar 1923	June 1923	July 1923	Aug 1923	Sept 1923	Oct 1923	Nov 1923

Price of bread (in marks), 1922–1923

Effects of hyperinflation: People were paid by the hour so they could spend the money before it became worthless, bartering became common, pensions became worthless, the poor became even poorer, the rich, land owners and anyone with large debts thrived.

After the Wall Street Crash of 1929, all Germans suffered economic problems. Businesses failed, wages decreased by an average of 60% and some industrial areas had an unemployment rate of over 50%.

How did the Great Depression weaken the Weimar government?
* The government became unpopular as it responded by raising taxes, cutting wages and cutting benefits.
* President Hindenburg took control of the Reichstag.
* The public saw the government as weak and started to look towards stronger leadership.

Quick Test

1. Why did the German public hate the War Guilt Clause so much?
2. Who were the 'November criminals'?
3. What did the government do in response to the economic issues of the early 1920s?
4. Give two reasons why the Great Depression was bad for the Weimar Republic.

Nazi rise to power, 1929–1933

Rise to power, to 1933

For much of the 1920s, the Nazis were a tiny minority party in the Reichstag. In 1928 they polled 2% of the overall vote. This all changed with the 1929 Wall Street Crash and ensuing Depression.

1930	• President Hindenburg ruled using Article 48. • The public lost faith in the government and turned to more extreme parties. • Communist support rose. Rich businessmen feared for their futures, so offered financial support to the Nazis. • 14 September – the Nazis polled over 18% of the vote.
1931	• Nazis increasingly popular, demonstrating organisation at a time of chaos, offering solutions to all Germany's problems. They deliberately disrupted Reichstag proceedings to make the government look weaker.
1932	• Hitler received 13 million votes in the Presidential election to Hindenburg's 19 million. • A series of weak Chancellors made Hitler look an increasingly viable candidate.

Date of Election	May 1928	Sep 1930	Jul 1932	Nov 1932	Mar 1933
Communists (KPD/USPD)	54	77	89	101	81
SPD (Social Democrats)	153	143	133	121	120
Centre Party (Catholics)	62	68	75	70	74
DDP (Democrats)	25	20	4	2	5
Right-wing parties (BVP/DVP/DNVP)	134	90	66	83	72
NSDAP (Nazis)	12	107	230	196	288
Others	51	72	11	12	7
Total Deputies	491	577	608	584	647

Election results 1928–1933

By 1933 Hindenburg was aged 85 and desperate. The Depression was deepening, the country was in chaos and there were few options left. As a result, Hitler was appointed Chancellor on 30 January 1933.

Consolidation of power, 1933–1934

In February 1933, the Reichstag building was set on fire. A Dutch Communist, van der Lubbe, was arrested and charged with starting the fire. That night, 4000 Communist leaders were arrested and imprisoned. Hitler persuaded Hindenburg to pass an emergency law suspending all the articles in the Constitution, including freedoms of speech, the press and assembly. The emergency law also:

- Gave police powers to search houses, confiscate property and detain people without trial.
- Decreed the death penalty for a wide range of crimes.
- Gave the police power to ban meetings, close newspapers, round up political opponents and send them to concentration camps.

The public turned against the Communists and, in the March election, the Nazis achieved their best ever election results. However, they did not have an overall majority. Hitler realised that he would need even more drastic action.

The Nazis launched a campaign of propaganda showing how all other parties (especially the Communists) were a threat to Germany. Hitler filled the cabinet with Nazis and other supporters. The SA and SS bullied non-Nazis into supporting them. This gave Hitler the chance to pass more laws.

THINK POINT

There were short-term and long-term factors that led to Hitler becoming Führer. Which factor do you think was the most important? Can you support your answer?

Enabling Act, March 1933	Gave Hitler freedom to pass laws without consulting Parliament. Made him legal dictator.
Power of local government destroyed	Meant that everything was controlled by the Nazis. Trade unions were banned.
Law against the Formation of New Parties – July 1933	SA attacked opposition parties' headquarters and arrested party members. Germany became a one-party state.
Destroyed the legal system	Hitler set up the 'People's Court', which tried 'enemies of the state' for treason.

Three more steps ensured that Hitler had total control.

- The 'Night of the Long Knives' (29–30 June 1934). The SS arrested and executed Ernst Röhm and 400 SA members. This removed any opposition from within the Nazi party and guaranteed loyalty to Hitler.
- President Hindenburg died aged 86 (2 August 1934). Hitler merged the position of President and Chancellor.
- All members of the army swore an oath of loyalty to Hitler as Führer.

Quick Test

1. Give two reasons why the Nazis had grown in popularity by 1931.
2. How old was President Hindenburg when he appointed Hitler Chancellor?
3. Why was the Reichstag Fire important for the Nazis?
4. Why was the Enabling Act important for Hitler?

Nazi control

The structure of Nazi Germany was military and military-style obedience was required. Germany was no longer a democracy and there was no freedom of speech or association.

Who helped Hitler control Germany?

SA (or Brown Shirts)	• Paramilitary wing of the Nazi party, led by Ernst Röhm. • Helped introduce organisation in time of chaos and bullied opponents. • Purged in the Night of the Long Knives.
SS (or Black Shirts)	• Totally loyal bodyguards of Hitler. • Controlled intelligence, security and police forces. • Carried out the extermination of 'undesirables'. • Executed SA in the Night of the Long Knives.
Gestapo (Secret State Police)	• Aimed to eliminate political opponents. • Responsible for the rounding up of Jews during the Nazi regime.
'People's Courts'	• Set up to try opponents to the Nazi regime. • Resulted in thousands being sent to concentration camps.
Propaganda	• Nazis controlled newspapers, films and radio in order to spread their message. Josef Goebbels was in charge of Nazi propaganda. • Culminated in the annual Nuremberg Rallies.
Concentration camps	• Used in order to hold political prisoners and as a method of control. • Inmates were used as forced labour. Jews, criminals, homosexuals, gypsies, the mentally ill and others were sent there by 1939.

Treatment of Jews and other groups

1933	• Jewish shops attacked by SA troops. • April – one-day boycott of Jewish businesses. • Jewish doctors and dentists forbidden from working in state hospitals; Jewish lawyers and teachers sacked. • Non-Aryan editors removed from German newspapers. • Law passed to sterilise up to 350000 men and women including Jews, gypsies, Jehovah's Witnesses and disabled people.
1934	• Special edition of *Der Stürmer* published reviving the accusation that Jews kill Christian children. • All homosexuals banned from military service.

TOP TIP

Look at some of the many Holocaust education websites to find out more about how the Nazis persecuted Jews and other opponents.

1935	• Jews and all non-Aryans excluded from military service. Jews prevented from becoming officers in the army.
	• The Nuremberg Laws passed
	– Jews and gypsies no longer citizens of Germany.
	– Marriage and relationships between Aryans and non-Aryans forbidden.
1936	• Jewish families not entitled to state benefits (e.g. child allowance).
	• 400 gypsies taken to Dachau concentration camp.
1937	• Jews banned from working in any government or political role.
1938	• Red 'J' stamped on all Jewish passports.
	• Kristallnacht
	– 1000 synagogues set alight; 7000 Jewish businesses destroyed
	– 20 000 Jews sent to concentration camps
	– Nearly 100 Jewish men murdered.
1939	• Law passed to allow Jews to be taken to camps for forced labour.
	• October – first Jewish ghetto established.
	• 3000 gypsies sent to concentration camps.

Opposition in Nazi Germany

Socialists were one of the largest groups to speak out. Many socialists were employed by the state, so were dealt with through the Enabling Act. They struggled in the face of SA/SS force and refused to collaborate with the Communists, so any real threat was reduced.

Communists also opposed the Nazis, but with little success. Many were arrested and executed after the Reichstag Fire and the party was banned by the end of 1933.

The Church influenced the German public and was therefore seen as a more serious threat to Nazi control. Hitler knew that crushing the Church would be unpopular, so tried to work with them:

• Concordat with Catholic Church signed in 1933, guaranteeing each side would stay out of the other's business.
• Protestant churches joined together in one official Reich Church in September 1933.
• National Reich Church set up in November 1933. *Mein Kampf* replaced the Bible and the Swastika replaced the cross.

Bishop Galen and Pastor Martin Niemöller were two church leaders who spoke out. Niemöller was arrested and put in solitary confinement for seven years.

Quick Test

1. What were the methods of control in Nazi Germany?
2. What were the Nuremberg Laws?
3. Who was in charge of propaganda?
4. What happened to Pastor Niemöller?

Nazi social and economic policies

Methods to ensure support from ordinary people

Throughout the Nazi regime, it was clear that winning the public over was the main way to maintain control. Thus, Hitler aimed to keep the people on his side through delivering on his promise to make Germany a great nation again.

- The Nazis aimed for full employment through suspending reparation repayments, reinvesting the money in German companies and making Germany self-sustaining. Thousands were employed by the government building hospitals, schools and motorways. National Service employed all able young men for a time. Women and Jews were sacked, so there were more jobs for 'real' German men. Hitler ignored the Treaty of Versailles and rearmament created jobs in industry.

- There was financial help for families. For example, money was given for couples to marry (a loan of 1000 marks) and each child born was given 250 marks.

- Hitler believed that militarism was the key to success. It was essential that Germany should have a strong leader. This was the 'Führer Prinzip' – one person should have all the power to make all the decisions. All Germans had to learn to trust and obey the Führer without thinking. People had to ignore their own self-interests and put Germany before themselves. They had to be willing to suffer or sacrifice themselves if it benefited Germany. The importance of war was highlighted, as Hitler wanted people to believe that only through war could the Master Race expand and get *Lebensraum* (living space).

- The Nuremberg Rallies were held every summer and were a chance for Hitler to show his military power to Germans and to the rest of the world. The rallies took place in the Nuremberg Arena and included fireworks displays, torch lit processions and military marches. The highlight of the week of rallies was Hitler's speech, in which Hitler appeared like a military god. The rallies displayed the Nazis' military values and might.

A poster for the League of German Girls

DID YOU KNOW?

Schemes were launched in order to help German citizens and increase Nazi popularity. For example, Volkswagen cars, camps and cruises were offered at a reduced rate. Rewards such as these are often called the 'carrot' when punishments are the 'stick'. Draw a diagram showing how the Nazis controlled the German people by using rewards and punishments.

How did the Nazis control the young?

Hitler believed that the Nazi regime could only be sustained by bringing up young Germans to be 'good' Nazis. Youth organisations and education were a key part of controlling the Nazi future.

The Hitler Youth movements were set up in 1925 and by 1936 there were over four million members. All other youth organisations were banned. The youth organisations were key in controlling the rest of the population. Members were encouraged to inform their leaders about other children and adults who were not living in the 'Nazi way'.

Boys	Girls
The army of the future in order to secure a 'Thousand Year Reich'.	Expected to provide future generations of soldiers and to ensure that children were brought up in the 'Nazi way'.
Expected to join the Hitler Youth from the ages of 14 to 18. Prior to that were the 'Little Fellows' from 6–10 and the 'Youth Folk' from 14–18.	Expected to join the League of German Maidens.
Encouraged to learn military techniques and take part in military training.	Encouraged to take part in physical activity in order to make them fit for motherhood.

How did the Nazis control education?

Schools were to follow Nazi ideology, with any opposition teachers removed very quickly. Pupils were brainwashed at any opportunity. Maths textbooks referred to bombing of Jewish ghettos and asked pupils to calculate the cost of keeping mentally ill Germans alive.

Schools had the military discipline of the youth movements. Head teachers were given more power to punish pupils and complete obedience was expected from all. Physical Education and History were key subjects for boys, while girls studied Eugenics (racial science) and Home Economics, which included motherhood and bringing up children.

Teacher points to Danzig explaining its strategic importance to the Nazis

Quick Test

1. Give three examples of ways in which Hitler increased male employment.
2. What was the purpose of the Hitler Youth movements?
3. What subjects did girls focus on at school?
4. How was education altered to deliver the Nazi message?

Timeline

1918 – Kaiser abdicates and First World War is over.

1919 – Spartacist Revolt.

1923 – Munich Beerhall Putsch.

1929 – Wall Street Crash and the beginning of the Great Depression.

January 1933 – Hitler appointed Chancellor of Germany.

February 1933 – Reichstag Fire.

June 1934 – Night of the Long Knives.

August 1934 – Death of President Hindenburg.

1935 – Nuremberg Laws introduced.

1938 – Kristallnacht.

1939 – First Jewish ghetto established.

Biographies

Adolf Hitler (1889–1945)

Born in Austria, Hitler became leader of Germany in 1933 and ruled until he committed suicide in 1945. He was a failed artist, a soldier in the First World War and leader of the Nazi party from 1921. Hitler was a skilled public speaker and strong leader. He held very strong anti-Semitic beliefs and saw it as his mission to rid Europe of Jews and make Germany great again. He sought revenge for the loss of the First World War and believed that the German people were destined to dominate Europe.

Josef Goebbels (1897–1945)

Goebbels was in charge of propaganda in Nazi Germany from 1933–1945. Through his aggressive use of propaganda, he made Hitler and the Nazis appear to be the only solution to Germany's problems. He campaigned against the Socialists and Communists as well as Jews. From 1933 he had total control over all areas of the media. He produced several anti-Semitic films and was responsible for the events of Kristallnacht. Goebbels committed suicide at the end of the Second World War.

Heinrich Himmler (1900–1945)

Himmler was a member of the Nazi party from the early 1920s, having served as a soldier in the First World War. He became head of the SS in 1929 and was elected to the Reichstag in 1930. He became head of the police state in Nazi Germany and set up the first concentration camp in Dachau in 1933. He was in charge of making Germany 'racially pure' and he oversaw the attempt to exterminate all Jews in Europe. Himmler was captured by the Allies at the end of the Second World War, but committed suicide while in custody.

Paul von Hindenburg (1847–1934)

Hindenburg served as Germany's President from 1925 to his death in 1934. He was a First World War hero and remained President throughout some of Germany's most difficult times. He appointed Hitler in 1933 through desperation. A series of failed governments had left him with little choice. When Hindenburg died, Hitler merged the posts of Chancellor and President.

Friedrich (Martin) Niemöller (1892–1984)

Pastor Niemöller was a sailor in the German Navy during the First World War. When the war ended, Niemöller became a preacher. He rejected the new Weimar government and supported some of the right-wing parties in Germany. Initially, he spoke favourably about Hitler and the Nazi Party, but later was very outspoken in his criticism of their anti-Jewish policies and founded the Confessional Church. He was imprisoned in Dachau and Sachsenhausen concentration camps from 1937–1945.

Immigration to 1928

Throughout the nineteenth century, the USA had an 'open door' policy towards immigration. Immigrants were welcome to make their fortune in the 'New World'.

The USA at the end of the First World War

By 1920 the population of the USA had grown to over 100 million people, with thousands flooding in through this 'open door'.

At first, the majority were from north-west Europe (Britain, France, Germany and Scandinavia). These 'old immigrants' were White Anglo-Saxon Protestants (WASPs). 'New immigrants' from Poland, Italy and Russia started arriving by 1900. By the end of the First World War there were more 'new immigrants' from India, China, Japan, Africa and the Middle East.

With the First World War far away in Europe (America joined the war late in 1917), the USA had escaped the worst of the horrors of war. Industry

Immigrants at Ellis Island

and agriculture grew and America replaced Britain as the 'workshop of the world'. It was an attractive country with a good climate, plenty of jobs and a welcome for all immigrants. It was a place where hard work would be rewarded with riches – a place where you could live the 'American Dream'.

What was the status of the ethnic groups in the USA?

New immigrants – the first wave

The first wave of new immigrants faced fewer issues than other ethnic minorities. Initially they were welcomed into American society, but hostility grew as their numbers increased and they were accused of stealing jobs. The Second World War raised awareness of them being outsiders and there was significant hostility, especially towards Italians (and Germans).

These new immigrants tended to settle in cheaper areas of housing in the cities. The Jewish and Roman Catholic immigrants were targeted by the **Ku Klux Klan (KKK)** from 1915 and were accused of being Communists.

They were never denied political rights and so were able to make more progress than other minorities. They were able to integrate more fully into American society due to their physical appearance and the colour of their skin.

Hispanics

They lived in *barrios* – slum areas with poor living conditions. They were separated by language and religion. They often worked in very poorly paid agricultural jobs and were seen by white Americans to be stealing jobs and lowering wages.

Asians

Asians arrived in huge numbers from the mid-nineteenth century due to the discovery of gold in California and faced significant discrimination. There were anti-Chinese riots in San Francisco as early as 1877.

They faced significant hostility during the Second World War when Japan and the USA fought over the Pacific. Much of the Japanese population in America was put in concentration camps.

Native Americans

The tribes of Native Americans historically conflicted with white Americans. They lost large areas of land and were forcibly removed from prosperous areas and moved to reservations. They were denied the right to vote and were not granted citizenship of the USA until 1924.

Black Americans

At the bottom of the racial hierarchy due to the history of slavery in the USA, black Americans faced 'de jure' (legal) segregation in the south. Separate facilities and schools existed and overt racial abuse was common.

They faced 'de facto' (not legal, but happened all the same) segregation in the North. Living in the poorest ghettos of the northern cities, black Americans had very few educational opportunities and they often worked in the poorest paid jobs.

THINK POINT

If you have ever moved home, what has been the reason? Do you know if your ancestors moved? The Ellis Island website is excellent and you can find out whether any of your ancestors emigrated to America.

Quick Test

1. What does 'WASP' stand for?
2. Where did most new immigrants come from?
3. Why was the Second World War important for new immigrants?
4. What is the difference between 'de jure' and 'de facto'?

'Separate but equal', to 1945

'Jim Crow Laws'

'Jim Crow Laws' were introduced between 1870 and 1900; one of the best known is the 'Separate but Equal' Act of 1876.

- Black children were forbidden to attend schools with white children.
- Black Americans had restricted access to parks and restaurants.
- Black Americans were not allowed to marry white Americans.
- There were even separate graveyards and bathrooms.

These laws basically made racism in the south legal and made it very difficult for black Americans to improve their situation.

Segregated drinking fountain

How did attitudes towards immigration change in the 1920s?

In the early 1920s two key laws were passed that illustrate the changing attitude of Americans towards immigration.

1921 Emergency Immigration Act

- Introduced a quota that severely restricted immigration from non-WASP countries. Under the quota system 80% of those entering came from Britain, Ireland, Germany, Holland, Switzerland and Scandinavia.

1924 National Origins Act

- Set an absolute limit of 150000 immigrants per annum and sharply restricted immigration from the south and east of Europe and Asia.

Why did attitudes towards immigration change in the 1920s?

The nature of immigration changed

By the end of the nineteenth century, the number of new immigrants arriving was greater than the number of old immigrants. This threatened the WASP way of life. Also, many of the new immigrants were Roman Catholic or Jewish, which threatened the Protestant establishment. Many came from non-democratic countries. This was seen as a threat to the US Constitution. Most did not speak English and so were seen to be less intelligent.

First World War

The First World War had led to hostility towards anything foreign and in 1917 the US closed its borders to immigrants. War created tension with the large German-American population. Italians were also targeted and anti-Japanese racism peaked at this time.

Internal conditions

WASPs feared that the number of immigrants would threaten employment, education and housing. The new immigrants' willingness to work for very low wages led to tension, as they were often used as strike-breakers.

Attitudes towards immigration changed as a result of a combination of factors. However, it is clear that the threat felt by the WASP establishment is the key to explaining the restriction on immigration. As a result of this threat, some started to look for extreme solutions to problems of immigration and extreme violent organisations like the KKK re-emerged.

Migration to the north

Social and economic conditions in the south led many African Americans to migrate to the northern states where it was believed economic opportunities were better. However, when they arrived, African Americans found that segregation existed in the shape of ghettos in the city and that racism still existed.

What was the Ku Klux Klan?

- Based mainly in the southern states.
- Often members were policemen, lawyers, judges and politicians, which made them difficult to oppose. Influential votes would be lost if the government acted against them.
- Dressed in white robes and hooded masks; used the burning cross as a symbol.
- Lynched black Americans they thought were trying to challenge the status quo; prevented black Americans from voting in elections.

KKK march in New Jersey

Many black Americans moved to the northern cities to escape persecution. KKK activity moved north as a result of this 'Great Migration'.

TOP TIP

The activities of the KKK are often seen as a cause of discrimination. Actually, the KKK is a symptom of discrimination already in place. Some historians argue that WASPs feared for their status in America, so the violence, including murder, beatings and arson, was a reaction to that fear.

What was the impact of KKK activity?

- Ensured black Americans were unable to change the situation in the southern states.
- Ensured that segregation and racial abuse carried on.
- Kept up pressure on the government not to introduce change.

Quick Test

1. Which groups of immigrants were restricted in the 1920s?
2. In what ways did the First World War have an impact on immigration?
3. What steps did the KKK take in order to maintain WASP superiority?
4. Why would the government not want to stop the KKK?

Civil rights movement, 1945–1968

Why did the civil rights movement grow at this time?

Impact of the Second World War

Black American soldiers talked about the 'Double-V-Campaign': victory in the war and victory for civil rights at home. Philip Randolf (an early leader in the movement) demanded an end to segregation in the armed forces. Executive order 8802 achieved this.

Organised resistance

Despite some improvement in black Americans' civil rights, the Jim Crow Laws continued across the south. Discrimination after the Second World War meant that an organised movement was needed in order to improve the situation.

Two key areas demonstrate the link between the discrimination and an organised movement:

Education:

- 1954 – Brown *v* Board of Education of Topeka. The National Association for the Advancement of Colored People (NAACP) supported the case that tried to allow a black child to go to a 'white' school.

- 1957 – Little Rock Central High School. The NAACP supported nine black students in their attempt to go to Little Rock Central High School.

Protest against the integration of Little Rock High School, 1959

Transport:

- 1955 – Rosa Parks and the Montgomery Bus Boycott. This started with Rosa Parks refusing to give up her seat on a bus for a white person. Supported by the NAACP, there was an organised bus boycott in Montgomery. This resulted in buses being desegregated.

Public awareness

Two key events attracted much publicity:

Emmett Till murder (1955)

- 14 year old Emmett Till was brutally murdered for speaking to a white woman in Mississippi. Pictures of his beaten body sparked outrage.

- The case attracted widespread publicity and proved just how much an organised civil rights movement was needed.

Birmingham Sunday School bombing (1963)

- Four children were killed by a large explosion in a Baptist Church.

- Following the bombing there were violent clashes between protestors and the police.

- Again this violence against black Americans made the call for civil rights louder.

GOT IT? ☐ ☐ ☐   **Free at Last? Civil Rights in the USA, 1918–1968**

Emergence of effective black leaders

The best known of these leaders was Martin Luther King. King believed that non-violence was the key to achieving civil rights. He was an inspirational leader, great organiser and powerful speaker. He led boycotts, sit-ins, freedom rides and marches, such as the 300 000-strong march on Washington.

Effective black organisations formed

- NAACP – key in many of the early protests.
- The **Southern Christian Leadership Conference (SCLC)** – organised march on Washington and protests in Birmingham.
- The Student Nonviolent Coordinating Committee (SNCC) – played a major role in organising sit-ins and freedom rides.
- The Congress of Racial Equality **(CORE)** – also helped organise the march on Washington and the freedom rides.

What was the federal and state response?

- Peaceful actions were met with violent retaliation.
- Leaders such as Bull Connor and Governor Wallace used clubs, fire hoses and police dogs to control the protestors.
- President Kennedy reacted by introducing the 1964 Civil Rights Act.

What was the impact on US society?

The combined efforts of civil rights groups ultimately resulted in the 1964 Civil Rights Act and the 1965 Voting Rights Act, which granted:

- Equal voting rights for black Americans.
- An end to discrimination on the basis of colour of skin in public buildings and the workplace.
- An end to segregated public schools.

However:

- Racism was still widespread across the southern states.
- King wanted further change.
- Very few black Americans had succeeded in registering to vote (especially in Alabama).

> **DID YOU KNOW?**
>
> Some of the first civil rights leaders like Marcus Garvey suggested that the best way to improve the position of black Americans was to leave America and return to Africa.

Quick Test

1. What was the 'Double-V-Campaign'?
2. Why were cases like the murder of Emmett Till important?
3. What did Martin Luther King believe would bring about change?
4. Why was the 1964 Civil Rights Act important for black Americans?

Ghettos and black American radicalism

What were ghettos?

Most black Americans lived in run-down, slum areas of the cities, known as ghettos.

The ghettos grew as a result of the Great Migration in the 1950s and 1960s. Thousands of black Americans moved north to escape the problems in the southern states and to find homes and jobs in the northern cities.

Race riots

Watts, Los Angeles (1965)

- The population was 98% black, but the police force was almost entirely white.
- The black population was growing impatient with the lack of progress of the civil rights movement, unemployment was high and poverty was reaching an unbearable state.
- A fight broke out that grew into a confrontation between police and black residents of Watts. The riots lasted for six days and left 34 dead, 900 wounded and 4000 arrested.

Watts riots, 1965

Chicago (1966)

- On 12 July police shut down a fire hydrant that had been opened by black teenagers wanting to cool down.
- A fight broke out in which ten people were injured, windows were smashed and some shops were looted.
- The next night saw sniper fire, petrol bombs and the stoning of city firemen.

Long hot summers (1966–1967)

- There were 43 race riots in 1966 and 159 in 1967.
- Black Americans in the northern cities were beginning to lose faith in non-violent protest and started to look to new leaders.

The northern civil rights movement

By the middle of the 1960s the civil rights movement was changing. Non-violence was becoming less popular and the northern cities wanted change. They looked towards more extreme leaders like Malcolm X and Stokely Carmichael.

Malcolm X's beliefs

- White and black societies should be totally separate.
- He was prepared to use violence.
- He showed hatred towards the white 'devils' in his speeches.

Stokely Carmichael

- Elected national chairman of SNCC in June 1966.
- He was an advocate of black supremacy and 'black power'.
- He left the SNCC in 1968 to join an even more extreme group called the Black Panthers.

> **TOP TIP**
>
> It is important to look at the differences between the movement in the north and in the south. Draw a table showing the differing views of Martin Luther King and Malcolm X.

How did the government respond to radical protest?

The government launched an investigation into the violence and rioting. It was led by Otto Kerner, who discovered several things that shocked the nation.

- USA was divided into two societies – one black and poor, the other white and richer.
- 40% of all black Americans lived in poverty and this was the reason for the riots.
- Black men were twice as likely to be unemployed as white men.
- Black men were three times as likely to be in low-skilled jobs as white men.

What was the reaction to Kerner's findings?

Little was done in response to most of the findings of the Commission, but there was a significant step forward in regard to one of the major conclusions.

The new Civil Rights Act of 1968 was passed in direct response to the problem of poverty and acknowledged that there was a definite link between poverty and housing.

Quick Test

1. Why did black Americans move north in the Great Migration?
2. In which cities were there race riots in the 1960s?
3. What did Malcolm X believe would bring about change?
4. Why did the Kerner report shock people?

Timeline

- – Emergency Immigration Act passed.
- – Native Americans granted American citizenship.
- – Brown *v* Board of Education of Topeka.
- – Rosa Parks and the beginning of the bus boycotts in Alabama.
- – Little Rock High School.
- – March on Washington and the 'I have a dream' speech.
- – Civil Rights Act passed.
- – Malcolm X assassinated.
- – Martin Luther King Jr. assassinated.
- – Civil Rights Act passed.

Biographies

Martin Luther King Jr. (1929–1968)

Martin Luther King Jr. was probably the most famous civil rights leader anywhere in the world. He was a Baptist minister and winner of the Nobel Peace Prize in 1964. He was a key organiser of many of the civil rights movement's most important protests, such as the march on Washington in 1963. He also protested against the war in Vietnam, as it was against his belief in non-violence. King was assassinated in 1968.

Malcolm X (1925–1965)

Born Malcolm Little, he changed his surname to 'X' as a symbol of his slave ancestry. He converted to Islam after a spell in prison in the early 1950s. He later spoke of his regret about some of his actions as part of the 'Nation of Islam'. His speeches were full of suggestions that white people were the devil who should be kept separate from black society. Malcolm X was assassinated in 1965.

Stokely Carmichael (1941–1998)

Born in Trinidad in the Caribbean, Carmichael became an important civil rights leader working with Martin Luther King in the southern states. He later lost faith in non-violent tactics and moved towards the 'black power' movement, becoming associated with the violent Black Panthers. Carmichael left America in 1969 and lived the rest of his life in north-west Africa.

Rosa Parks (1913–2005)

Rosa Parks was a civil rights leader most famous for being arrested for refusing to give up her seat on a public bus in Montgomery, Alabama. She was supported by the NAACP and there followed a series of bus boycotts across the city. This was a key moment in the civil rights movement and involved Martin Luther King. Parks lived most of her life in Detroit working as a secretary to an African-American politician.

Marcus Garvey (1887–1940)

Garvey was a Jamaican born activist most famous for his 'Back to Africa' campaign. Garvey was highly intelligent and a talented public speaker. He formed the Universal Negro Improvement Association (UNIA) in 1914 and soon developed a reputation as a strong and inspirational leader. He founded the Black Star Line as a transport company to help black Americans return to Africa.

Reasons for the emergence of the Cold War

The Cold War is the name given to the period from 1945 to 1989 when suspicion and rivalry between the USA and her allies and the Soviet Union and her allies threatened armed conflict.

The Iron Curtain

TOP TIP

Become familiar with the terms that relate to the Cold War. An understanding and the correct use of terms such as communism and capitalism will impress an examiner.

In a speech in 1946, the former British Prime Minister, Winston Churchill, talked about an 'Iron Curtain', an imaginary barrier between the democratic countries in the West and the Soviet dominated communist countries in the East. The phrase meant that the East and West were deeply divided by different beliefs.

Capitalism: USA	Communism: Soviet Union
Industries/businesses privately owned.	Industries/businesses owned by the state.
Individual ambition and the creation of wealth encouraged.	Wealth shared equally.
Choice of several political parties.	One-party state – only the Communist Party allowed.
Free speech and debate.	Only communist ideas promoted. Government cannot be challenged.

Reasons for breakdown of relations

TOP TIP

Political terms relating to the Soviet Union can be tricky. Background reading on twentieth century Russian history will help you understand your study of the Cold War, e.g. the Red Flag chapter.

- Stalin created a buffer zone of communist countries to prevent the USSR from being attacked. By 1948 the USSR controlled almost all of Eastern Europe.
- **Truman Doctrine:** proposed that the USA would lend money to any country to fight communism.
- **Marshall Plan:** offered aid to European countries to rebuild after the war.
- **Berlin airlift:** In 1945 the British, Americans, French and the Russians each controlled one area or zone of Germany. The capital, Berlin, which was inside the Russian zone, was also divided into four zones. In 1948 Stalin ordered the blockade of all roads, railways and canals leading into West Berlin. American and British planes flew in supplies to keep the people in West Berlin alive. The Berlin airlift was a turning point in the relationship between East and West. The Western powers joined their zones to form the Federal Republic of Germany or West Germany while the Russian zone became the German Democratic Republic or East Germany.

- Two alliance systems developed. In 1949 a number of Western nations set up the **North Atlantic Treaty Organisation** (NATO) to protect them from the USSR. If one member was attacked, the other members would help them. The Soviet Union and its Eastern European allies responded with a similar alliance in 1955 called the **Warsaw Pact**.

Military rivalry

Due to mutual suspicion, each side built more weapons. Both the United States and the Soviet Union increased the size of their armies and air forces. The arms race became more dangerous when each side began to develop bigger and more destructive nuclear weapons. The build-up of nuclear arms increased tensions even more.

The Arms Race	
1945	USA drops two atomic bombs (A-bombs) on Hiroshima and Nagasaki in Japan.
1949	Soviet Union explodes its first A-bomb.
1952	USA explodes a hydrogen bomb (H-bomb).
1955	Soviet Union tests its first hydrogen bomb.
1957	Soviet Union tests its first intercontinental ballistic missile (ICBM) capable of carrying a nuclear missile.

The Cold War now had the potential to turn into a devastating world war. A state of mutually assured destruction (MAD) had been reached.

The Korean War

In 1945, Korea split into North and South, with the North being communist and the South being non-communist. In 1950, North Korea invaded South Korea. The USA, worried about the potential spread of communism, got the United Nations to send in troops to help South Korea. There was some initial success with General MacArthur's troops conquering most of North Korea, but in 1950 the Chinese army helped to recapture the North and push the US troops south. Both sides reached an impasse at the North/South divide – the 38th parallel. There were continued clashes until President Eisenhower offered peace to the Chinese or use of the atomic bomb if they refused.

Quick Test

1.   What was the 'Cold War'?
2.   What action was taken by Stalin to prevent the Soviet Union from being attacked?
3.   What event marked a turning point in the relationship between the East and the West?
4.   What was the aim of the North Atlantic Treaty Organisation?

Cold War flashpoints

Poland and Hungary, 1956

Stalin died in 1953 and Nikita Khrushchev became the new leader of the Soviet Union. In 1956 Khrushchev criticised Stalin's rule. Some Warsaw Pact countries hoped there might be a relaxation of Soviet control.

- Workers in Poland protested against Soviet domination and demanded political reform. The demonstrations were suppressed but Poland gained some reforms as long as they remained loyal to the USSR.
- There were also demands for reform in Hungary culminating in Imre Nagy's threat to leave the Warsaw Pact. Soviet tanks entered Budapest to put down the uprising. Around 20 000 Hungarian people were killed and thousands fled abroad.

Berlin

A divided Berlin presented problems for the USSR:

- It was the only place in Eastern Europe where people in communist countries had contact with the West. East Berliners saw that West Berliners had a higher standard of living and more freedoms.
- Many East Germans moved to the West through Berlin. Many were skilled workers, which created a labour shortage in East Germany.

In 1961, Khrushchev ordered the building of a wall to cut Berlin in two with barbed wire and guard towers to prevent anyone escaping to the West. The 'Iron Curtain' was now a physical reality.

The West protested and sent extra troops to West Berlin. However, the possibility of war had been reduced between the two superpowers.

- The flood of refugees from the East came to a halt, although people still tried to escape and were killed in the attempt.
- The Soviet Union abandoned its attempts to force Western troops out of Berlin.

Construction of the Berlin Wall

Cuba, 1962

- In 1959, Batista was overthrown by revolutionaries led by Fidel Castro. The USA imposed sanctions after Castro took control of American businesses in Cuba.
- US President Kennedy approved a CIA plan for an invasion at the Bay of Pigs. The invasion was a failure and humiliated Kennedy.
- Castro formed an alliance with the Soviet Union.
- On 16 October 1962, a US spy plane revealed evidence of Soviet missile launch sites being built on Cuba.
- On 22 October, the USA imposed a naval blockade of Cuba to prevent Soviet ships landing missiles.
- Kennedy stated that a missile attack from Cuba would result in a full-scale attack by the USA on the USSR.
- Kennedy began to mobilise troops for a possible invasion of Cuba. The world feared a nuclear war between the two superpowers.

The crisis came to an end on 28 October.

- Secret negotiations were held between Kennedy and Khrushchev.
- Despite a US spy plane being shot down over Cuba and the US navy searching a Soviet merchant ship for missiles, neither side took action.
- Kennedy ended the blockade and promised not to invade Cuba.
- In a secret deal between the two leaders, the Soviet Union agreed to remove their missiles from Cuba in exchange for the removal of US missiles from Britain, Italy and Turkey.

The Cuban Missile Crisis had an important impact on international relations and led to a thaw in the Cold War.

- Telephone 'hot line' between Washington and Moscow set up in 1963.
- Test Ban Treaty signed, agreeing to stop all nuclear tests in the air, under water or in space.

Quick Test

1. Who replaced Stalin as the new leader of the Soviet Union?
2. Why did Soviet troops move into Budapest?
3. Why did the Soviet Union order a wall to be built separating East and West Berlin?
4. What actions were taken by the USA after evidence was discovered of the presence of Soviet missiles on Cuba?

The Vietnam War

Reasons for United States' involvement

In 1954, the people of Vietnam won their freedom from French rule. The north became a communist republic under the control of the Viet Minh, led by Ho Chi Minh. The south became an anti-communist republic under Ngo Dinh Diem. In the late 1950s communist guerrillas (the Vietcong) in South Vietnam began fighting Diem's government, which was unpopular and corrupt. North Vietnam sent weapons and soldiers to help the Vietcong while the United States sent weapons and advisers to the South Vietnamese. By 1964 the USA had become involved in a full-scale war. The main reasons were:

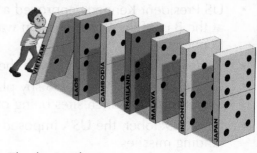

The domino theory

- The situation in Vietnam provided an opportunity to make a stand against communism.
- The USA believed in the 'domino theory'. This was the belief that if South Vietnam fell to the communists, other countries would follow suit.
- North Vietnam received help from China and the USSR. The USA feared the possibility of a new communist superpower bloc.

Reasons for the failure to defeat the Vietcong

By 1973 US troops had withdrawn from Vietnam, ultimately unable to defeat the Vietcong. The reasons for this were:

- The Vietcong were experienced in guerrilla tactics. They were also hard to spot as they did not wear uniforms and lived among the peasants.
- The North Vietnamese built the Ho Chi Minh Trail to supply South Vietnam with troops and equipment.
- In contrast, American tactics proved ineffective.
- American soldiers were not trained or equipped for jungle warfare. Low morale sometimes resulted in excessive drinking and drug use. Due to the draft system, the American army mainly consisted of inexperienced young conscripts.

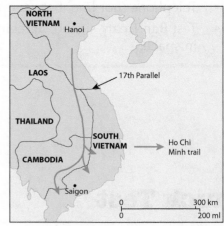

The Ho Chi Minh Trail

Tactic	Reasons for failure
Bombing of strategic targets such as army bases and railways.	Bombs often missed their targets. Children and hospital patients were among those killed.
Peasants were moved from their villages and placed in **strategic hamlets** to prevent contact with the Vietcong.	Resulted in the Vietnamese peasants hating the Americans.
Chemical bombs including **napalm** were used to destroy trees in the jungle.	Innocent civilians, men, women and children were burned by napalm.

Changing views on the war in the USA

Why did the Vietnam War become increasingly unpopular in the United States?

- It was costing billions of dollars. Hundreds of thousands of American soldiers lost their lives. Television coverage showed the full horrors of the war. The American people became demoralised by atrocities such as the My Lai massacre.
- Tactics such as the use of napalm and Agent Orange turned people against the war.

How did the American people show their opposition to the Vietnam War?

- Large demonstrations and student protests.
- Draft dodging.
- Vietnam veterans and famous figures such as Mohammed Ali and Martin Luther King spoke out against the war.
- Anti-Vietnam songs were popular.

Impact of the Vietnam War on international relations

In 1975 South Vietnam was invaded and defeated by North Vietnam. Vietnam was unified as a single communist country. American involvement in Vietnam was largely seen as a failure, not only by the American public, but internationally.

TOP TIP

Although Laos and Cambodia became communist, other countries in South East Asia, such as Thailand, did not. The domino theory had been proved wrong. Some people argue that the domino theory was just an excuse for the USA to increase its power.

Quick Test

1. What was the 'domino theory'?
2. What was the Ho Chi Minh Trail?
3. Why was there low morale among American soldiers?
4. Why did public opinion in America turn against involvement in Vietnam?

Changing relations between the superpowers, 1968–1989

Attempts at détente

Throughout the 1960s and 1970s the USA and the USSR tried to put aside their differences. They formed a détente, or understanding, with each other that reduced tension and the threat of war. The reasons for the changing attitudes between the USA and the USSR were:

- The Cuban Missile Crisis had shown how close they had come to nuclear war.
- Better relations meant fewer weapons needed to be built. This allowed Western and Eastern leaders to portray themselves as peacemakers and increase their popularity. There were anti-nuclear demonstrations in a number of countries.
- The USA had economic problems. Money spent on nuclear weapons meant there was less available to improve living conditions.
- The USSR also faced economic problems. It was spending 20% of its budget on defence. Its industry was also very inefficient compared with American industry. Soviet industry had to improve before people's standards of living could rise.
- The USSR had begun to quarrel with communist China.

Several agreements were made to improve relations between the USA and the Soviet Union.

- In 1972, the SALT I Treaty led to a reduction of nuclear weapons.
- In 1975, 33 European countries signed the Helsinki Agreement confirming the existing borders of Europe.

There were also trade links between the superpowers and co-operation over space missions.

Setbacks

However, a number of events led to the breakdown of détente by the late 1970s and early 1980s.

- In 1979, Soviet forces invaded Afghanistan.
- In 1980, the new American President, Ronald Reagan, referred to the Soviet Union as 'the evil empire'.
- The USA boycotted the Olympic Games in Moscow in 1980 and the Soviet Union boycotted the 1984 Los Angeles Olympic Games.
- The USA increased its defence budget and announced the Strategic Defence Initiative, which proposed satellite systems that would be able to shoot down Soviet missiles before they hit their target.

End of the Cold War

In 1985 Mikhail Gorbachev took power in the Soviet Union. Gorbachev wanted to reform communism and address the social, economic and political problems within the Soviet Union. He proposed to do this through a combination of:

Germans on top of the Berlin Wall as it is torn down

- **Glasnost** meaning openness or a free exchange of ideas and information. The press had more freedom, criticism of the government was tolerated and previously banned books could be read.

- **Perestroika** meaning a reconstruction of the entire Soviet system. Gorbachev relaxed state control of industry in the hope that the Soviet economy would become more productive.

In 1987 a landmark agreement between the Soviet Union and the USA removed all nuclear missiles from Europe and reduced the number of ICBM missiles. This agreement effectively brought the arms race to an end.

Gorbachev also began to change the Soviet Union's role in Eastern Europe. Warsaw Pact countries were given more independence. By 1989 several European countries had rejected communism. In November 1989 the Berlin Wall was torn down. This was a key moment in the history of Europe and symbolised the end of the Cold War.

> **THINK POINT**
>
> Was the Cold War a struggle between different belief systems, communism and capitalism, or was it a struggle for power? Historians continue to debate explanations for the Cold War between the East and the West from 1945 to 1989.

Quick Test

1. What was meant by 'détente'?
2. What actions were taken by the superpowers to improve relations?
3. Who was the American president who referred to the Soviet Union as an 'evil empire'?
4. What were Gorbachev's two ideas for reforming communism?

Timeline

May 1945 – The Second World War in Europe comes to an end.

12 March 1947 – US President Truman promises to resist communism.

29 August 1949 – The Soviet Union carries out its first atom bomb test.

November 1952 – The USA explodes its first hydrogen bomb.

November 1956 – Soviet troops invade Hungary to suppress an anti-communist uprising.

13 August 1961 – Construction of the Berlin Wall begins, dividing the city in two.

October 1962 – The Cuban Missile Crisis brings the world to the brink of nuclear war.

8 March 1965 – The USA sends marines to fight communist-led guerrillas in Vietnam.

8 December 1987 – The signing of a nuclear arms treaty signals the end of hostile relations between the USA and the Soviet Union.

9 November 1989 – Gates in the Berlin Wall are opened as communism collapses in Eastern Europe.

Biographies

Mikhail Gorbachev (1931–)

Mikhail Gorbachev was leader of the Soviet Union from 1985 to 1991. He came to agreements with the USA to reduce the numbers of nuclear weapons and withdrew Soviet forces from Eastern European countries and Afghanistan. Two of his most important policies were *perestroika* (restructuring) and *glasnost* (openness).

Ronald Reagan (1911–2004)

US President from 1980 to 1988, Reagan was determined to stand up to the Soviet Union. Reagan increased American spending on nuclear missiles. His policy towards the Soviet Union changed in the late 1980s when he met with Mikhail Gorbachev to discuss limiting the number of nuclear weapons countries owned.

Nikita Khrushchev (1895–1971)

Khrushchev was the leader of the Soviet Union from 1953 to 1964. In 1956 he criticised Stalin at a Communist Party congress. In 1962 he placed Soviet nuclear missiles on the island of Cuba, which brought the USA and the Soviet Union close to war.

John F. Kennedy (1917–1963)

Kennedy was US President from 1960 until his assassination in 1963. He took a tough line towards the Soviet Union over West Berlin. In 1962 he negotiated with Khrushchev to avoid a nuclear conflict during the Cuban Missile Crisis.

Joseph Stalin (1879–1953)

Stalin was Soviet leader from 1929 to 1953. Stalin's brutal dictatorship of the Soviet Union led to the deaths of millions of Soviet citizens. After 1945 Stalin extended Soviet influence to Eastern Europe. In 1948–49 Stalin tried to remove the Western allies from West Berlin through the Berlin blockade.

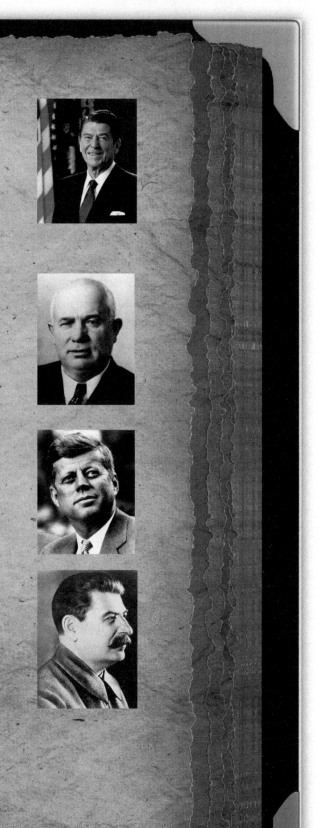

Exam skills

Describe question

Describe questions are designed to test your knowledge of an event. The questions should be relatively straightforward as long as you have done some revision before trying to answer the question. The question will start with the word 'Describe'.

Describe the conditions the soldiers faced in the trenches.

Or

Describe the stages of the Triangular Trade route.

Key points

- These questions are worth 4 marks.
- You will probably be asked to describe an event, like the Battle of Bannockburn, or a development, such as the impact of World War One on Scottish women.
- One relevant point = one sentence = one mark.
- Four relevant points are required.
- The points you make do not have to be in any particular order, but should make sense.
- You will be positively marked, i.e. you will not have marks deducted for anything you get wrong. You will be credited for everything you get right, as long as you answer the question being asked.

In order to successfully complete the answer:

- Give information that directly answers the question.
- You will need to have revised. It is important that you know enough detail about key events, and their effects and key people, and impacts they made.
- You can get more marks for developing points by giving further information and adding more detail to your point. However, this must be linked to the question. An example of this can be found below.

Example question

Describe the events of the Munich Putsch in November 1923.   **4 marks**

You need 4 pieces of information describing what happened during the Munich Putsch.

Answer 1

> *Hitler attempted to seize power in Munich and take over the Bavarian Government. This was called the Munich Putsch. It was when he tried to take power in Germany.*

Markers' comments

This candidate has clearly answered in 3 sentences. However, there is only one real point that answers the question. The candidate has said what the Munich Putsch was but has not described the details of the event in particular. This is a good lesson for the candidate to learn before the actual exam, they need to provide more detail of the Putsch itself to be credited with marks.

Answer 2

In November 1923, Hitler attempted to seize power in Munich and overthrow the Bavarian government. He did this by storming into the Burgerbraukeller in Munich and fired a shot from his gun declaring 'the national revolution has broken out!' He forced von Kahr, von Lossow and von Seisser to support the revolution at gun point. Hitler also got the crowd in the Beer Hall to support the coup. The next day, the Nazi troops met with the army in the street and fighting broke out. Sixteen Nazis were killed in the fighting and Hitler himself was injured, he hurt his shoulder and had to flee whilst the army restored order to the streets.

Markers' comments

This scores full marks. The candidate has written more than the 4 required points and has clearly described the events of the Munich Putsch. The candidate has written a description of what happened at each stage and has therefore been credited with a mark for each point made.

Explain question

These questions ask you to explain why an event or change happened. They are worth 6 marks. You will recognise them because they will start with the word 'explain.' There is no set way to answer these questions, but there are some basic rules.

Key points

In order to successfully complete the answer:

- You need to write at least 6 sentences – one for each mark.
- You get a mark for each point you make relevant to the question. A further mark is available for developing points.
- Each point you make must be linked to the question – there must be a clear link between the information and the issue in question.
- You must do more than just DESCRIBE the issue/situation/change.
- A good idea is to start each point you make on a new line, and count your points numerically. For example:

One reason…

A second reason…

A third reason…

And so on. This makes it easy for you to see how many points you have written down – and for the examiner!

Example question

Explain the reasons why many Scottish men enlisted in the army during World War 1. **6 marks**

Answer 1

There were many reasons why men joined up during WW1. Men joined because they wanted a holiday and money. The men were excited for war and wanted to fight the Germans, most men thought they were cruel and needed taught a lesson. Men were happy to fight in the trenches as it was less boring than being at home.

Markers' comments

Answer 1 is a weak answer despite giving some relevant points. The points are only loosely linked to the question and would benefit from being more structured, clearly linking each point back to the question, explaining why it was a reason men enlisted during WW1. This is a common mistake, as candidates often give factors that relate to the question but without explaining the link to the question. For example, the first point that 'Men wanted a holiday and money' would be better written 'Men joined up because of unemployment at home, joining the army gave them an opportunity to earn money.'

Answer 2

One reason why Scottish men enlisted in the army was because of unemployment at home, joining the army gave men an opportunity to earn money.

A second reason why men enlisted was because of the initial excitement when war was announced – war fever captured the enthusiasm of many men and they rushed to join up.

A third reason why men enlisted was because of propaganda. Posters asked men to join up and sometimes there was anti-German propaganda to stir up patriotic feeling to encourage enlistment.

A fourth reason why men joined up was because of the 'white feather'. Women would pin a white feather on men who hadn't joined up, and rather than be labelled a coward they enlisted instead.

A fifth reason men joined up was they thought it would be a short war; it would be 'over by Christmas'. Many men did not want to miss the opportunity to travel and fight before the war had ended.

A sixth reason men enlisted was because of conscription. This was introduced in 1916, stating all men aged 18–41 were to join up if asked, largely because numbers of volunteers had reduced to almost nothing.

Markers' comments

Answer 2 is a much stronger answer as it is well structured with each point clearly detailed and linked back to the question. It does not just describe reasons why men enlisted. This answer would receive full marks.

To what extent/How important/How successful question ... or the '9 marker'.

This type of question requires you to make a judgement about a particular issue. You are required to give a balanced answer after making a judgement about the relative importance or success of other relevant factors and come to a reasoned conclusion.

Key points
- This type of question is worth 9 marks.
- 1 mark is awarded for your introduction.
- Up to 5 marks can be gained for relevant points of knowledge. 1 mark will be awarded for each separate correct and relevant point. However, a maximum of 3 marks will be awarded if only one factor is discussed.

- 2 marks are awarded for your conclusion – one mark for a judgement or summarising the reasons you have discussed and one mark for a reason in support of the judgement.
- 1 mark for your information being presented in a structured way (with knowledge being organised in support of different factors).

Example question

How important were the actions of William Wilberforce in the campaign to abolish the slave trade?   **9 marks**

Answer 1

William Wilberforce was important in helping the abolition of the slave trade as he worked in Parliament to have it abolished.

William Wilberforce was a key politician who campaigned for nearly 20 years to have the slave trade abolished. He introduced petitions and a bill nearly every year to persuade the other members of parliament to pass the bill abolishing the slave trade. Wilberforce was helped by Thomas Clarkson.

Overall, Wilberforce was the most important reason why the slave trade ended as he persuaded Parliament.

Markers' comments

The answer begins by addressing the isolated factor in the question but does not introduce any other factors, indicating that Wilberforce did not act alone.

The candidate then goes on to describe what Wilberforce did in Parliament to help Abolish the trade. The candidate does bring in Thomas Clarkson as another abolitionist but fails to give any further information on why his contributions were important.

Finally, the candidate just offers a brief summary sentence to agree with the question being asked, although they do give a reason to support their judgement.

This answer requires much more detail in terms of the OTHER REASONS (in this case the other abolitionists) that contributed towards the end of the slave trade.

Answer 2

Certainly, the actions of William Wilberforce were very important when assessing the reasons why the slave trade was abolished. He was a leading politician so was able to bring the argument to Parliament. However, there are many other reasons why the slave trade was abolished, such as the work of Thomas Clarkson, and Olaudah Equiano.

William Wilberforce was a key politician who worked for 20 years to abolish the slave trade in Parliament. He introduced a bill almost every year to attempt to end the trade, even though he was fighting against many MPs who wanted to keep the trade. Eventually, Wilberforce was successful, the Bill being passed into law in 1807. Therefore, Wilberforce was important because he did not give up until the bill was passed.

However, Wilberforce was supported heavily by the work of Thomas Clarkson. Clarkson worked extremely hard to gather evidence to show the cruel treatment of the slaves – from the way they were kept on board during the middle passage to the horrendous punishments they faced. 'Clarkson's chest' contained artefacts like thumbscrews that Wilberforce was able to use in Parliament to prove the cruelty of the trade. Further, Clarkson interviewed 20 000 sailors to gather enough evidence to prove the horrible conditions on the middle passage. Thus, Thomas

Clarkson is also very important in the abolishment of the trade as without his evidence Parliament might not have known how cruel the trade actually was.

Olaudah Equiano was also important. Equiano was an ex-slave whose personal testimony was vital evidence in the cruel treatment of human beings taken from Africa. He was able to detail his life from being kidnapped in Africa, the Middle Passage and life on the plantations to show how cruel the slave trade was. Wilberforce was able to use this evidence and the public also found out about how cruel the trade was, which meant they too gave their support to end the trade. Therefore, Equiano is very important.

Overall, William Wilberforce was important in the campaign to end the slave trade, however so were Clarkson and Equiano. On balance, it would be fair to judge that Clarkson was perhaps more important than Wilberforce as without the huge amount of evidence Clarkson had gathered, Wilberforce would not have been able to persuade the other politicians in Parliament to pass the bill.

Markers' comments

This is a much more comprehensive, well-structured and detailed answer. The candidate has started by addressing the question, stating the Wilberforce was important and gone on to list some other factors they will cover.

They have separated the information into 3 paragraphs, which makes it easy to read and understand – this helps them to gain a structure mark.

The information about each factor is detailed and they link each factor back to the question at the end of each section – stating how important they think each factor is.

In the conclusion, the candidate summarises the individual factors in list form and makes a judgement over the isolated factor, supporting their judgement with a valid reason.

This answer would receive the full 9 marks.

Evaluate the usefulness of a source

This question asks you to evaluate whether a source is useful for learning about an event or period in history. Evaluate the usefulness questions will always be worth 5 marks.

Key points

In order to successfully complete the answer you must comment on:

* **Provenance**

  This means **when** the source was produced, **who** produced the source and **why the source was produced**.

  In the exam, up to **4 marks** are available for this section.

  In order to gain the marks for the section on Provenance it is not enough to simply identify who wrote it, when it was written or why it was written. You **must** include an **evaluative comment** that shows how useful the source is.

* **Content**

  This means **what** the source is about. You need to make a comment on the detail contained in the source and then make an **evaluative comment** on how useful the information is in relation to the question, commenting on whether or not is accurate.

  There are **2 marks** available for this section.

- **Content omission**

  This means **what** the source has **omitted – what it does not tell you**.

  It is important that you use **specific recall** to illustrate content omission.

  There are **2 marks** available for this section.

As you will have noticed, it means that you do not have to get the full marks available for each of the above areas to get full marks for the question.

Following a simple formula might help you answer this question and achieve the full range of marks on offer.

A useful formula might be:

SODAP

Source

Omission

DAte

Purpose

If you cover one point for each of the things above correctly then you could achieve full marks.

Example question

Source A is from a book by a railway inspector, published in 1870

> The comforts, or rather discomforts, of railway travelling abut thirty years ago were very different from those of the present day. Third-class carriages were often little different from basic cattle trucks. For a considerable time they were completely open and had no seats. First and second class carriages were covered and had seating. The luggage of the passengers was packed on top of the carriages.

Evaluate the usefulness of **Source A** as evidence of railway travel in the nineteenth century.   **5 marks**

(You may want to comment on who wrote it, when they wrote it, what they say or what has been missed out.)

Answer 1

> *Source A is quite useful. It is a primary source from 1870 which is at the time of the event. It was written to inform us of what rail travel was like in the nineteenth century. The source tells us that rail travel has got better as people do not have to sit in open carriages. The source does not tell us how fast trains could go by 1870.*

Markers' comments

Answer 1 makes some mistakes that you must try to avoid:

- It fails to use the language of the question – there is no reference to how useful the source is, each point made needs to refer back to the usefulness of the source to show the examiner you have engaged with the question.

- It does not accurately refer to the event taking place – it makes a general and vague comment about this being written 'at the time of the event'. You must be specific to gain a mark.

- The recall is not specific enough to receive a mark – you would have to make a comment on what speed trains could go by the late nineteenth century to merit a mark.

Answer 2

Source A is only partly useful as evidence of railway travel in the nineteenth century. The source mentions that earlier in the century third class carriages were often little different from basic cattle trucks. This is accurate as third class carriages were often little more than open boxes, this makes the source more useful. Another point the source tells us is that the first and second class carriages were covered, had seating and their luggage was carried on top. This is accurate as first and second class carriages definitely had roofs; this makes the source more useful. However, the source is less useful because it does not contain full information about rail travel in the nineteenth century. It fails to state that railway travel grew more popular because it was much cheaper and quicker than coach and canal travel; this makes the source less useful. Another point of omission is that the railways linked up important towns and cities so people could export goods for trade easily and also travel for work and leisure, this makes the source less useful. The source is more useful as it was written in 1870, making this a primary source from the time of rail travel in the nineteenth century. The source was written by a railway inspector who will have had first-hand experience of observing the trains and railways, making it more useful. The purpose of the source is to inform of the improvements that had been made to rail travel by 1870, making it more useful as he was an eyewitness to rail travel.

Markers' comments

This is a full and detailed answer that has used the SODAP formula to help cover the key points as follows:

- The candidate identifies two points of detail from the source, describes them and confirms them as **accurate**, which makes the source useful. You MUST do this to achieve the marks. Two marks would be awarded here.
- The candidate then successfully describes two points of omission, stating that this makes the source less useful because they are relevant points that have been left out. You MUST do this to achieve the marks. Two marks would be awarded for this section.
- The candidate comments on the date being useful, stating it is useful because it was written at the time of rail travel – they have been specific and not just said 'the time of the event'. This is needed to achieve the mark. They also comment that this was a primary source.
- The candidate then comments on the usefulness of the author, explaining that their job gave them first-hand experience.
- Finally, the candidate tells us why the purpose of the source is useful; bringing in that the author was an eyewitness to events.

The candidate clearly has written 7–8 marks worth here so would achieve the full 5 marks available.

Top tips:

- Keep relating each point you make to the USEFULNESS of the source.
- Every source is useful to a certain extent – what you are being asked to do is to decide *how* useful it is.

- Primary sources are useful because they were written at the time the event being asked about in the question; the author more often than not was present at the event taking place or experienced it in some way. Comment on this!
- Secondary sources are useful because they are written years after the event being asked about, which gives the benefit of hindsight; they are often written by historians who will have researched the topic being asked about thoroughly.

Source comparison question

This question requires you to compare the views of two sources overall and in detail.

Key points
- The question is worth 4 marks.

In order to successfully complete the answer:
- When comparing the sources overall you must describe what they agree or disagree about without quoting. There are up to 2 marks available for overall comparisons.
- When comparing the sources in detail you must use specific examples supported by quotations. There are up to 2 marks available for direct comparisons.

Example question

Source A describes the Battle of Loos.

The Battle of Loos was fought in September 1915. On September 25th the British 1st Army commanded by Douglas Haig attacked German positions at Loos. Haig's plan was simple – concentrated British artillery fire and pinpoint infantry fire would give the advancing British troops sufficient cover. In the lead up to the attack, another weapon became available to Haig – poison gas. He realised that such a weapon would neutralise the German machine gunners. The British lost many men to German machine gun fire as they attacked German positions around Loos without the aid of artillery support. The battle effectively ended on September 28th. The British suffered 50 000 casualties while the Germans lost about 25 000 men.

[Adapted from http://www.historylearningsite.co.uk/battle_of_loos.htm]

Source B describes the Battle of Loos.

The Battle of Loos formed a part of the wider Artois-Loos Offensive conducted by the French and British in autumn 1915. Presided over by Douglas Haig, the British committed six divisions to the attack. Haig's battle plans called for the release of 5100 cylinders of chlorine gas from the British front line. During the battle the British suffered 50 000 casualties. German casualties were estimated much lower, at approximately half the British total. The British failure at Loos contributed to Haig's replacement of French as Commander-in-Chief at the close of 1915.

[Adapted from http://www.firstworldwar.com/battles/loos.htm]

Compare the views of Sources A and B on the Battle of Loos. **4 marks**

Answer 1

The sources agree. They are both describing the Battle of Loos. Source A says it was fought in autumn 1915 and Source B says it was in September 1915. Source A says that they used poison gas and source B says they used chlorine gas. Both sources say that the British lost 50 000 men.

Markers' comments

Answer 1 is very basic in its approach. The overall comparison does not describe the views of the sources, only what they describe. It does not use the language of the question and it offers basic comparisons without developing the point.

Answer 2

Sources A and B agree about the Battle of Loos. The sources agree that the British were commanded by Douglas Haig and agree about the tactics he used during the battle. They also agree that the British suffered heavy losses during the battle.

The sources agree that the battle took place in autumn 1915. Source A writes 'The Battle of Loos was fought in 1915', Source B agrees by writing 'The Battle of Loos formed a part of the wider Artois-Loos Offensive conducted by the French and British in autumn 1915.' The sources further agree that the British were commanded by Douglas Haig: Source A states 'the British 1st Army commanded by Douglas Haig attacked German positions at Loos' and Source B agrees by writing 'Presided over by Douglas Haig, the British committed six divisions to the attack'. The sources also agree that Haig used poison gas: Source A writes 'In the lead up to the attack, another weapon became available to Haig – poison gas' and source B writes 'Haig's battle plans called for the release of 5100 cylinders of chlorine gas from the British front line'. The sources also agree that the British suffered much heavier losses than the Germans. Source A writes 'The British suffered 50 000 casualties while the Germans lost about 25 000 men' and source B agrees by writing 'During the battle the British suffered 50 000 casualties. German casualties were estimated much lower, at approximately half the British total.'

Markers' comments

Answer 2 is much more successful than answer 1. It consistently uses the language of the question and successfully compares the source overall and in detail. When it gives direct comparisons it develops the point by stating what they agree about, and then quotes to support the point.

How fully does source? question

This question requires you to make a judgement about the extent to which a source provides a full explanation or description of an event or development.

Key points
- A How fully? question will ask 'How fully does source ... explain ...?' or 'How fully does source ... describe ...?'
- The source you are asked to evaluate will contain four points relevant to the question but the source will also contain information that is not relevant to the question. It is important that you read both the question and source carefully.

- A **How fully?** question is worth 6 marks. You can receive up to 3 marks for identifying points from the source that supports your judgement – this is where you have to be careful, considering whether the information you have selected from the source links correctly with what is being asked in the question, especially for 'explain'.
- You can receive up to 4 marks for points of omission.
- Note that this adds up to a potential 7/6. So you could still gain 6/6 for 2 points from the source and 4 points from recall.
- However, a maximum of 2 marks may be given for answers in which no judgement has been made or which refer solely to the source.
- The judgement itself is not worth any marks, but you MUST have one to be eligible for the full range of marks on offer.

In order to successfully complete the answer:

- Read the source carefully and make a judgement about how fully the source describes/explains the event or development in the question. For example, **The source describes/explains ... quite well.**
- Identify and interpret what the source tells you about the event or development. For example, **The source states that ...**
- Identify what important information the source does **not** mention. For example, **The source, however, does not mention that ...**

Example question

Source A is about some of the problems facing Mary, Queen of Scots in 1561 and is adapted from *The Kings and Queens of Scotland* by Richard Oram (The History Press).

> Mary's welcome lasted for several days with music and merrymaking. Most were delighted to have their young queen back to rule in person. However some Scots doubted Mary's ability to rule due to her youth and lack of experience. A minority of leading religious reformers including John Knox feared that Mary's return would upset the progress of the Scottish Reformation. Her insistence in maintaining her Catholic faith had to be explained. Mary also had to concede to the wishes of those Scots who now worshipped in the Protestant manner.

How fully does Source A describe the problems Mary, Queen of Scots faced when she arrived in Scotland in 1561?   **6 marks**

Answer 1

Source A says that some Scots doubted Mary's ability to rule as she was young and did not have a lot of experience in governing a country. The source states that Protestant leaders like John Knox did not trust Mary and thought she would try to put an end to the Scottish Reformation. The source also says her insistence in maintaining her Catholic faith had to be explained. Mary also had to concede to the wishes of those Scots who now worshipped in the Protestant manner.

Markers' comments

Answer 1 contains no judgement about how fully the source describes the problems facing Mary in 1561. Four points have been identified from the source. These four points are all relevant to the question. However, only the first two points have been interpreted. The other two points have merely been copied. No points of omission have been included. Due to the answer only referring to the source and the lack of a judgement, 2 marks only would be given for this.

Answer 2

Source A partly describes the problems facing Mary, Queen of Scots on her return to Scotland in 1561. Source A mentions how some Scots did not believe Mary could rule Scotland properly due to the fact she was young and inexperienced. The source also mentions how Protestant reformers such as John Knox did not welcome Mary's return to Scotland as they were worried she would interfere with the Protestant Reformation. The source also states how Mary insisted on worshipping the Catholic religion when Scotland had become a Protestant country. However Source A does not mention that some Scots were suspicious that Mary had been brought up in France and the French were unpopular with many Scots. Another important point not mentioned in Source A is that Mary now ruled over a religiously divided country. While Protestants did not want Mary to undo the Reformation, Catholics hoped Mary would restore the Catholic faith. Lastly, another problem facing Mary not mentioned in the source is that Elizabeth of England was suspicious of Mary after Mary claimed to be Queen of England.

Markers' comments

Answer 2 is a much stronger answer. There is a clear overall judgement at the beginning of the answer as to how fully the source describes the problems facing Mary, Queen of Scots in 1561. Three problems facing Mary are identified from the source. Each point is dealt with separately. These points are interpreted rather than simply being copied or listed from the source. There is therefore an understanding of the points being selected to support the judgement made at the beginning of the answer. In addition three good points of knowledge are made to support the candidate's judgement. This is a good answer, which would gain full marks.

The assignment

The assignment – background information

What is the assignment?

In total there are 100 marks available to you in History. The exam is worth 80 marks and the assignment is worth 20.

The assignment makes up 20% of your final mark.

The assignment tests your skills, knowledge and understanding. The assignment also gives you a chance to be challenged and to apply your skills and knowledge.

The best part of this assignment is that you get to choose your own topics to research and write about.

Your teacher can advise you on questions but cannot pick one for you. This is your piece of work.

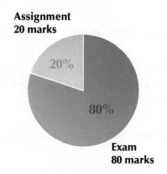

Assignment
20 marks

20%

80%

Exam
80 marks

What do I need to do?

You will get up to eight hours to choose a topic and question, plan out your assignment and also do your research.

At the end of this time you need to gather all your thoughts on to a single page of A4. This is your History Resource Sheet.

You will take this sheet into a room with you where, under controlled exam conditions, you will be given one hour to write up your assignment as an essay.

You can write as much as you want (or can) in the hour. There is no minimum or maximum word limit.

So what do I do now?

Choose a topic you have been studying and which you have enjoyed and would like to find out more about. Decide on a historical issue or question. It is all very well liking a topic but real history is about questioning, debating and analysing. So you will need to come up with a question.

This might seem quite hard but there is help at hand. Look at sample or old exam papers for the essay questions. These questions are ones that the SQA have approved, so they are good questions to use.

You can choose any question you like but it might be a good idea to choose a question on one of the topics you have been studying as it will deepen your knowledge before the exam.

Good questions and ones to avoid

❌ Lenin and the Russian Revolution

This is not a question but just a topic area. Any essay would be a story and not a historical analysis.

❌ To what extent did the use of gas at the Battle of Loos reduce the confidence of Scottish soldiers in gas as a weapon for the rest of the Great War?

The assignment

This is a historical question but it is very detailed and is one for which you might struggle to find source material to write a whole essay on.

❌ Was the Gestapo Hitler's most effective instrument of terror and how did he get into power?

This is a two-part question and makes it difficult for you as you would be trying to answer two questions at the same time.

✅ How far can it be argued that Martin Luther King was responsible for securing the 1968 Civil Rights Act?

This is an ideal question as you can mention Martin Luther King's contribution and also bring in other factors like Malcolm X's contribution, the Black Panthers, politicians' influence and other factors.

Some other good questions could include:

✅ How significant was Mary's marriage to Bothwell in leading to her downfall?

✅ To what extent was the potato famine of the 1840s the main reason for Irish immigration to Scotland in the nineteenth century?

✅ How far can it be argued that the First World War improved the economy of Scotland?

✅ How significant was the work of the colonial government in explaining the reasons for Scottish emigration in the nineteenth century?

✅ To what extent was the effect of the French Revolution the main reason for the delay in the abolition of the slave trade?

✅ How important was the Royal Commission of 1842 in improving working conditions in the coal mines?

✅ How far can it be argued that the Labour Party successfully created a Welfare State?

✅ How far can it be argued that the personality of the Tsar was the most important reason why there was a revolution in Russia in February 1917?

✅ To what extent do the actions of the Gestapo explain the lack of successful opposition to Nazi control in 1930s Germany?

✅ How far can it be argued that the civil rights campaign under Martin Luther King was unsuccessful?

✅ How important was the role of Gorbachev in changing relations between the Superpowers, 1968–81?

Take a look back at the questions to avoid and what we have said about why they are difficult questions for the assignment. Have a think about how these questions might be improved on. What other questions might you ask about these topics? Jot down some ideas and look at past and sample papers to see if these are the sort of questions that will help you write a good historical analysis essay.

Planning the assignment

You will get to take a one page History Resource Sheet in with you when it is time to write up your assignment. Your Resource Sheet must contain no more than 200 words.

To help you get to that stage you will need to have a master plan of how you are going to attack your question. You will need to make sure that the question has lots of factors to discuss and analyse. Questions that start with 'To what extent …' or 'How far can it be argued ….' are good. Simple 'describe' questions do not give a chance for debate. For example:

To what extent did the Nazis' rise to power depend on propaganda?

Yes, propaganda

Also, unemployment

Also, appeal of uniform

Also, Nazi promise of employment

Also, conflict with Communists

Also, fear

Also, 'All Things to All Men'

For each question there will be a number of different areas you will want to explore as the diagram above shows. You will need to gather evidence under each area and will want to use different sources to gather that evidence. Each piece of evidence helps to **attack your question**.

You must use at least two different sources when you are researching the assignment.

To help gather all your research you might want to put together a folder with poly pockets or a sheet of paper for each factor you are going to explore. You can then write notes on each sheet or drop notes and post-its into the poly pocket.

Source checklist

- your jotter
- class textbooks
- library books
- ebooks
- websites
- TV documentaries
- history magazines
- local historians
- local sites, e.g. castles

Remember to take a note of which source you got each piece of information from (even if you put it in brackets after your notes). This is good practice to get into and you can mention in your essay where you got information from.

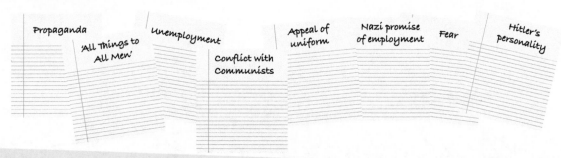

Propaganda / 'All Things to All Men' / Unemployment / Conflict with Communists / Appeal of uniform / Nazi promise of employment / Fear / Hitler's personality

TOP TIP

Your resource sheet must not go over 200 words. You also need to ensure that you do not include large 'chunks' of your essay in the resource sheet, for example, your entire introduction. However, you are allowed to write down a quote in full, you will not be penalised for this and in fact this is encouraged. To save on words, you can use acronyms, for example change Winston Spencer Churchill to WSC and World War One can be shortened to WW1. Try to use the resource sheet to help you remember the structure of your essay, the paragraphs and issues you are going to write about. You should also use it to remind yourself of key dates, statistics and key names.

The structure of the assignment

The assignment should look like an essay with an introduction, paragraphs on each factor in your essay and a conclusion. The illustration below shows the sort of structure it might take.

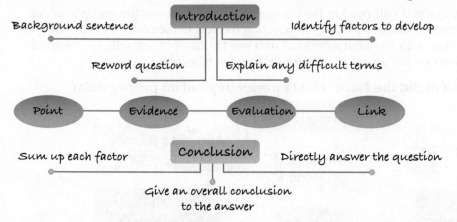

The above illustration shows that your introduction must set the question in context, explain terms that need further explanation and then shows all the factors you are going to develop in your essay.

Each paragraph should make a point, then give evidence to back it up. The writer (i.e. you) must then evaluate how important that point and evidence is. You should then write a sentence that links that paragraph back to the main question (almost like a mini conclusion for that section).

The conclusion must give a summary of the evidence, answer the question clearly, summarise each of the factors and use evidence from the main essay.

TOP TIP

Do not finish with a quote. It is your essay – you are the historian. If using quotes then make sure you use them to back up your arguments. Or, better still, argue against quotes of other historians. That is real history!

A checklist to help you

Did you?	Not done	Done	Done well	Self-assessment/ number of marks
Preparation				
Have I chosen an appropriate question and got it checked by my teacher?				☹ 😐 ☺
Have I developed a plan?				☹ 😐 ☺
Have I identified more than one source to research?				☹ 😐 ☺

National 5 Assignment Mark Scheme	Not done	Done	Done well	Self-assessment/ number of marks
A. Introducing the question or issue Select a question from the approved list or make sure your own has an 'isolated factor'. I have addressed the question, listed the factors I will cover and made a judgement.				/2
B. Using information from sources referred to, in order to support factors Use source evidence such as primary sources from people at the time or secondary sources such as quotes from historians in textbooks or statistics to support your knowledge.				/2
C. Using other knowledge to support factors Ensure you have detailed and clear knowledge on your main factor (in the question) and knowledge about additional factors to answer the question.				/4

D. Analysing the impact of different factors It is not enough to give detail on a factor you MUST analyse the importance/ significance of your main factors.				/3
E. Evaluating the overall impact of different factors You should make an evaluation comment on the main factors to sum up at the end of each paragraph – make a direct link back to the question.				/3
F. Organising the information to address the question or issue Order your essay in line with the question. Build argument throughout your essay.				/3
G. Coming to a conclusion that addresses the question or issue Make a relative judgement on the importance of your key factors.				/2
H. Supporting a conclusion with reasons Support your judgement with reasons.				/1
Total				**20**

Remember, you will not lose any marks for doing things wrong. Marking is always positive and you will be marked for what you have done well!

National 5
HISTORY

For SQA 2019 and beyond

Practice Papers

Colin Bagnall

Introduction

The exam

Your teachers and your class notes will have given you much of the factual information that you need to know about the topics and events in the various sections of the examination. If you feel that you need more information, there is much that you can find online to supplement these sources. You will also note that as a part of the mark schemes in this book there are suggestions for factual information that you might be expected to include. It is important that you are clear about the topics you will be answering on and that you have sufficient knowledge of these topics. There will be a Scottish topic, a British topic and a European and World topic for you to answer.

Don't be tempted to tackle a topic that you have not prepared for, even if you did see an amusing song relating to it on *Horrible Histories* the week before!

From 2018 the National 5 history exam will require a full coverage of skills and content. This means that you will get questions of a wider range of types in each section. There are more marks than in the first edition for using your knowledge and understanding, in particular to explain and evaluate what happened in the past. Most importantly it means that you will be in the examination room longer for the final exam than you would have been doing the exam in previous years – two hours and twenty minutes. You will also have only one minute per mark. It is very important to be organised and calm in the exam room: practice and preparation are everything.

Across the three topics you will be asked to address six types of question. Each requires something slightly different from you. The mark schemes point out the marker's expectations of your answer, but here is a brief outline:

1. **Describe something** – you don't need to worry too much about the order of what you write about and you should not use up valuable time explaining its importance or evaluating the role of various factors in your answer. You don't have to be entertaining. Stick to the facts that are relevant and write clearly. If there are four marks available, make four good points about the thing you were asked to describe and move on within five minutes.

TOP TIP Before you start, quickly write down on a scrap piece of paper five words or phrases that will work as headings for your description. This way you won't miss a point.

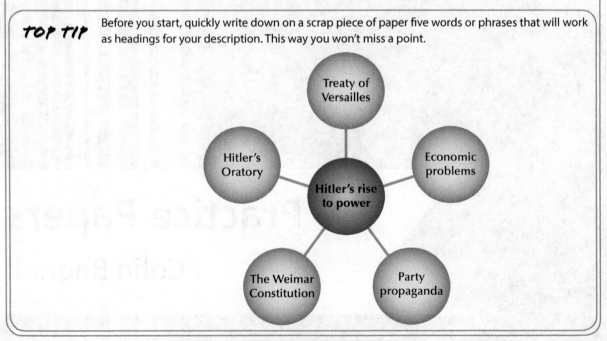

2. **Explain something** – this asks a bit more of you. You must show that you understand why something has occurred and make several different or related points that connect together into an explanation. You can get credit here if you expand one point into a larger point by saying more of significance about it. You don't need to say which part of your explanation was most important however. Again quickly add up your points to see if you have got all of the marks available. If there are 6 marks, you might have made six points, or you may have made three points, two of which you expanded enough to say they were worth 2 marks each. If there are 6 marks available move on after six minutes.

3. **Evaluate the extent to which a particular factor is important** – this asks a little more of you again. This time you have to identify the various factors in causing something and evaluate the relative importance of the one mentioned in the question. You should spend the most time on the factor mentioned; explain its significance against the others, which also have some importance.

TOP TIP   To help you picture the significance of a particular factor, try doing a 'ripple diagram'. Imagine the factor you are considering is like a stone dropped into a pond. It will have some immediate and obvious effects, then wider ripples, then, possibly longer-term consequences.

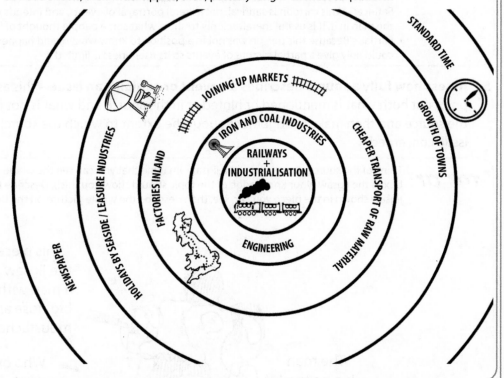

4. **Evaluate the usefulness of a source in helping you understand an issue or event** – a source-based question asks you to make a judgement about the reliability, value and validity of a source in relation to a specific event or issue. You can get marks for assessing the context or provenance of the source – who wrote it (or drew or photographed it, etc.), when it was created in relation to the events described, the purpose of the source – but also for the language used in the source and by accurately explaining what the source tells you about the issue or event.

TOP TIP

Have a bank of technical words ready for this type of question. Especially when you are trying to say in words whether a pictorial source is useful or not. Having to hand words that you are likely to use when answering this type of question under exam pressure is very helpful. For example:

- Propaganda – 'This poster is a piece of propaganda so it only shows one side of the story.'
- Exaggerated – 'The author of this article has used exaggerated language to make his point.'
- Biased – 'Because the writer here is writing about her deadly enemy she is biased in what she says.'
- Formal – 'This is a formal report of what happened, written in formal language, which makes it more reliable and therefore useful in finding out what happened.'
- Informal – 'Because this was a personal letter, it is not written formally so it is not very precise in what it says.'
- Official – 'This is the official account of what happened, so it is written by someone who was in a position to know what happened.'
- Private – 'This is a private diary, which was not for publication, so the author was being honest in what she said.'
- Public – 'This was for public consumption in a speech and does not reflect what he really thought about this issue.'
- Factual – 'The language used in this account is factual and so can be trusted as a reflection of what the author saw.'
- Opinion – 'This is a newspaper editorial which is simply expressing the opinion of the editor and he does not seem to provide many facts to support it.'
- Satirical – 'This cartoon is satirical, not a literal portrayal of events, and intends to make fun of the man in it. It is useful therefore only to show what some people thought of him.
- Partial – 'Because this person was not in a position to know what would happen the next day, it could only give a partial picture of events so its usefulness is limited.'

5. **Assess how fully a source describes an event or explains an issue** – this asks you to point out both what is mentioned or hinted at in the source and what is not mentioned in the source and then make a judgement about the extent to which the source addresses the issue concerned.

TOP TIP

Think of the source as one piece of a jigsaw. Imagine that you can see the whole picture on the box of the jigsaw (your knowledge of the topic should show you this!). Describe the parts of the jigsaw shown in the piece you can see, then describe the whole picture 'on the box'.

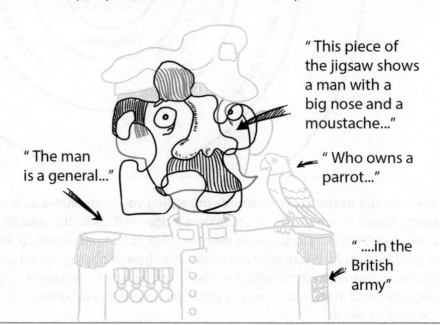

" This piece of the jigsaw shows a man with a big nose and a moustache…"

" The man is a general…"

" Who owns a parrot…"

" ….in the British army"

6. **Compare how two different sources view a particular event or issue** – this type of question requires you to make direct comparisons between the sources showing both agreement and differences with them. You should be able to find overall differences or similarities as well as smaller individual points.

TOP TIP Don't just write about one of the sources and then the other one. Make sure you make your comparisons direct ones.

Good luck! (Something that usually comes from preparation...)

Practice paper A

Practice Papers for SQA Exams

HISTORY
NATIONAL 5
Paper A
Reading for Understanding, Analysis and Evaluation

Duration – 2 hours and 20 minutes

Total marks – 80

SECTION 1 – SCOTTISH – 25 marks

Attempt ONE part.

SECTION 2 – BRITISH CONTEXTS – 26 marks

Attempt ONE part.

SECTION 3 – EUROPEAN AND WORLD – 29 marks

Attempt ONE part.

×Leckie
the education publisher
for Scotland

SECTION 1 – SCOTTISH – 25 marks

Attempt ONE part

Part 1 – The Wars of Independence, 1286–1328

Answer the following **five** questions using recalled knowledge and information from the sources where appropriate.

Source A are King Edward's words from the Treaty of Birgham of July 1290.

Source A

> We promise that the kingdom of Scotland shall remain separate and divided from the kingdom of England by its rightful boundaries and borders as has been observed up to now and that it shall be free and independent, reserving always the right of our lord or whoever has belonged to him.

1. Evaluate the usefulness of **Source A** as evidence of how Edward I became involved in Scottish affairs.

   (You may want to comment on who wrote it, when they wrote it, why they wrote it, what they say or what has been missed out.)

   5

2. Describe the role played by John Balliol during the Wars of Independence.

   4

3. Explain the reasons why William Wallace was able to organise resistance to Edward I.

   6

Source B is about the murder of Comyn and the crowning of Robert Bruce as King in 1306.

Source B

> Before committing such a crime in a church, Robert the Bruce had followed a cautious policy to protect his lands and power by supporting Edward I's rule in Scotland.
>
> It is hard to escape the conclusion that the murder of Comyn [led to] Bruce's seizure of the throne as he realised that his best chance of salvation lay in his becoming king, thereby drawing on the natural loyalty which attached to the cause of a legitimate monarch.

4. How fully does **Source B** explain why Bruce fought against Edward I and his son after 1306? (Use **Source B** and recall.)

   6

Sources C and **D** are about what happened after the Battle of Stirling Bridge.

Source C

Gradually, after Stirling Bridge, garrisons surrendered to Wallace leaving only Edinburgh, Roxburgh and Berwick in English hands. Wallace was knighted and appointed Guardian of the Realm. However, in 1297 old divisions in the leadership of Scotland came to the surface again when Wallace appointed William Lamberton as Bishop of St Andrews. Although many nobles were reluctant to follow him, most nobles and clergy accepted that he was the best hope to defend the Kingdom against Edward.

Source D

Wallace and Murray's startling victory at Stirling Bridge led to the almost immediate collapse of Edward's Military power in Scotland. Wallace was the hero of the hour. He was knighted, elected Guardian of the Realm in the name of King John and the Community of the Realm. He appointed his friend William Lamberton to be Bishop of St Andrews and all of Scotland's traditional leaders rallied to his side, with even those in prison in Flanders escaping to join him.

5. Compare the views of **Sources C** and **D** about the support for Wallace after the Battle of Stirling Bridge 1297. (Compare the sources overall and/or in detail.)   **4**

Part 5 – The Era of the Great War, 1910–1928

Answer the following **five** questions using recalled knowledge and information from the sources where appropriate.

Sources A and **B** are about recruitment at the start of the war.

Source A

Over 120 recruits for the Moray Firth Company of the Naval Brigade assembled in the Cluny Square under Lieutenant McLeod. In the presence of about 5000 the men were photographed. The men – brave, determined and eager for adventure – were conveyed by a splendid train, which left at 3.30 pm and as the train moved slowly out of the station, a thunderous roar of cheering rent the air. The scene was the most remarkable ever witnessed in the town.

Source B

When I went into the office on Monday morning a friend asked me, "What are you doing about the war?". Well I had thought nothing about it at all. He said, "Well, I have joined my brother's regiment. If you like, come along, I can get you in." At lunchtime I went to the recruitment office and there was my friend waiting for me. There was a queue of around a thousand people trying to enlist. But my friend came right along the queue, hauled me out and said, "Come along!" So I went right up to the front. I said I was eighteen and one month. "Do you mean nineteen and one month?", said the sergeant. I thought for a moment and said, "Yes Sir". He said, "Right-ho, well sign here, please".

1. Compare the views of **Sources A** and **B** about military recruitment at the start of the First World War. (Compare the sources overall and/or in detail.) **4**

Source C describes the use of tanks during the Battle of Cambrai 1917.

Source C

There were not enough infantry to take advantage of this huge hole in the German defences and the enemy soon began to recover and fight back. By evening many tanks had broken down – over a hundred from lack of petrol or engine failure and another sixty five from enemy gunfire, including sixteen knocked out by a single German field gun. All these tanks were now stranded in German territory and there were no reserves.

2. How fully does **Source C** describe the impact of tanks on war on the Western Front? (Use **Source C** and recall.) **6**

3. Describe the ways in which conscientious objectors were treated during the war. **4**

Source D is from a letter written by Emmeline Pankhurst to a Scottish Suffragette on 10 January 1913.

Source D

My Dear Friend

The Prime Minister has announced that the Women's Amendments to the Manhood Suffrage Bill will shortly be discussed in Parliament. The WSPU has declined to call any truce on its militant activities on the strength of the Prime Minister's promise to discuss the issue of votes for women. There is no commitment from the government to get the act carried. We must continue to show our determination. Women have been disappointed in the past. We will fight on and cause as much public disorder as we can. The cause is a just cause and it will triumph.

4. Evaluate the usefulness of **Source D** as evidence of the reasons why women won the vote in 1918.

   5

   (You may want to comment on who wrote it, when they wrote it, why they wrote it, what they say or what has been missed out.)

5. Explain the reasons why heavy industry declined in Scotland after the First World War.

   6

SECTION 2 – BRITISH CONTEXTS – 26 Marks

Attempt ONE part

Part 1 – The Creation of the Medieval Kingdoms, 1066–1406

Answer the following **four** questions using recalled knowledge and information from the sources where appropriate.

Source A was written by Gerald of Wales about King Henry II in his book *Concerning the instruction of a Prince*, which he wrote after Henry's death to explain what a good king was. He was a part of his court.

Source A

> He was a man of easy access and patient with those of lesser rank, flexible and witty, second to none in politeness ... Strenuous in warfare ... Very shrewd in civil life ... He was fierce towards those who remained untamed, but merciful towards the defeated, harsh to his servants, expansive towards strangers, spent generously in public, frugal in private... Humble, an oppressor of the nobility and a condemner of the proud.

1. Evaluate the usefulness of **Source A** as evidence of Henry's kingship.   **5**

   (You may wish to comment on who wrote it, when they wrote it, why they wrote it, what they say or what has been missed out.)

Source B

> Medieval Britain had very few towns and those that did exist were small by modern standards. In the middle ages most people were peasants who lived in villages. However religious centres appealed to many people, and some evolved into towns and cities. Hereford, Canterbury and Bath for example were Cathedral cities that attracted all kinds of people particularly traders and pilgrims. After the death of Thomas Becket in 1170 thousands journeyed to Canterbury each year on pilgrimage.

2. How fully does **Source B** explain the reasons why towns grew in the Middle Ages?   **6**

3. To what extent was the end of serfdom the most important consequence of the Black Death?   **9**

4. Explain the reasons why castles were built across Britain under Norman rule.   **6**

Part 5 – The Making of Modern Britain, 1880–1951

Answer the following **four** questions using recalled knowledge and information from the sources where appropriate.

Source A is from a modern history book.

Source A

Charles Booth, a Liverpool businessman published his first paper investigating poverty in Tower Hamlets in 1887, published in 17 volumes called 'The Life and Labour of the People of London'. Although his methods were flawed, he had shown a scale of poverty that could not be explained by the faults and mistakes of individuals. Rowntree's later study of poverty in York was much more carefully defined and illustrated clearly the different causes of poverty in Britain.

1. How fully does **Source A** explain why attitudes towards poverty changed in Britain in the late 1800s? (Use **Source A** and recall.)   **6**

2. To what extent did Liberal Welfare Reforms 1906–14 successfully address the problem of poverty in Britain in the early 20th century?   **9**

3. Explain the reasons why attitudes towards poverty in Britain changed during the Second World War.   **6**

Source B is from an editorial in a British newspaper from February 1948 and refers to Bevan's negotiations with doctors about pay and conditions in the new NHS.

Source B

The State medical service is part of the Socialist plot to convert Great Britain into a National Socialist economy. The doctors' stand is the first effective revolt of the professional classes against Socialist tyranny. There is nothing that Bevan or any other Socialist can do about it in the shape of Hitlerian coercion.

4. Evaluate the usefulness of **Source B** as evidence of reasons for the introduction of the NHS in 1948.   **5**

   (You may want to comment on who wrote it, when they wrote it, why they wrote it, what they say or what has been missed out.)

SECTION 3 – EUROPEAN AND WORLD – 29 marks

Attempt ONE part

Part 1 – The Cross and the Crescent: the Crusades, 1071–1192

Answer the following **five** questions using recalled knowledge and information from the sources where appropriate.

1. To what extent was the life of a medieval knight dangerous? **9**

Sources A and **B** are about the reasons why people went on the First Crusade.

Source A

Source A

> Pope Urban II at Clermont: This land you inhabit is everywhere shut in by the sea, is surrounded by ranges of mountains and is overcrowded by your numbers ... This is why you devour and fight one another, make war and even kill one another ... Let all dissensions [arguments] be settled. Take the road to the Holy Sepulchre, rescue that land from a dreadful race and rule over it yourselves.

Source B

> The preachers foretold confidently that the New Jerusalem would appear on earth when the Old Jerusalem was restored to Christian ownership. They spoke of a golden land, a land of milk and honey, where the rewards to those who helped to regain the Holy City for Christ would be immense.

2. Compare the views of **Sources A** and **B** about why people went on the First Crusade. (Compare the sources overall and/or in detail.) **4**

3. Describe the course of the People's Crusade. **4**

4. Explain the reasons for the fall of the Kingdom of Jerusalem to Saladin in 1187. **6**

Source C describes Richard I towards the end of the Third Crusade.

Source C

> During the winter, when Saladin had disbanded most of his forces, Richard took the army on an expedition into the hills. They got to within twelve miles of Jerusalem. But it was clear that even if they took the city, there was no way to hold it once Richard and his army had gone. If they entered Jerusalem and fulfilled their vows, few in his army would be inclined to stay. There were not enough Christian knights who wanted to live out their lives in the Holy Land. With the French King already departed and his brother plotting against him at home, Richard was looking for a way out.

5. How fully does **Source C** explain the problems facing Crusaders on the Third Crusade?   6

Part 4 – Hitler and Nazi Germany, 1919–1939

Answer the following **five** questions using recalled knowledge and information from the sources where appropriate.

1. Explain the reasons why there was opposition to the Weimar Republic in the early 1920s. **6**

Sources A and **B** are about the impact of the Great Depression on German politics.

Source A

Before the crash, 1.25 million people were unemployed in Germany. By the end of 1930 the figure had reached nearly 4 million, 15.3 per cent of the population ... wages also fell and those with full-time work had to survive on lower incomes. Hitler, who was considered a fool in 1928 when he predicted economic disaster, was now seen in a different light.

Source B

The Depression helped Hitler by undermining [German] democracy. The Republic was governed by coalitions because of the nature of the voting system. The Economic crisis caused the coalition under Muller to fall apart in 1930. The next three Chancellors ... relied on the President's powers ... to rule by decree without the support of the Reichstag. In this undemocratic atmosphere Hitler was able to come to power through the back door.

2. Compare the views of **Sources A** and **B** about the impact of the Great Depression on German politics. (Compare the sources overall and/or in detail.) **4**

3. Describe the treatment of minority groups in Germany by the Nazis in the 1930s. **4**

In **Source C** Hitler explains what he expects of young German men.

Source C

Young men must be strong and handsome. They must be fully trained in physical exercises. I intend to have an athletic youth – that is the first and chief thing. In this way I shall eradicate the thousands of years of human domestication. Then I shall have in front of me the pure and noble natural material. With that I can create the new order.

4. How fully does **Source C** explain Nazi policies towards young people in the 1930s? (Use the source and recall to reach a judgement.) **6**

5. To what extent was Nazi control of Germany due to propaganda? **9**

Practice paper B

Practice paper B

HISTORY
NATIONAL 5
Paper B
Reading for Understanding, Analysis and Evaluation

Duration – 2 hours and 20 minutes

Total marks – 80

SECTION 1 – SCOTTISH – 25 marks

Attempt ONE part.

SECTION 2 – BRITISH CONTEXTS – 26 marks

Attempt ONE part.

SECTION 3 – EUROPEAN AND WORLD – 29 marks

Attempt ONE part.

the education publisher
for Scotland

SECTION 1 – SCOTTISH – 25 marks

Attempt ONE part

Part 2 – Mary Queen of Scots and the Scottish Reformation, 1542–1587

Answer the following **five** questions using recalled knowledge and information from the sources where appropriate.

Source A is about the consequences of the Rough Wooing.

Source A

> The costs of the war are hard to assess. Government and society stood up well to seven years of garrisoning, forced quarter and violence. The Church suffered the most, but the effects were mixed: the occupation had greatly accelerated the spread of Protestant literature, which would later be blamed ... as the principal cause of the spread of heresy (reformation ideas), but collaboration with the English had also helped to drive the movement underground.

1. How fully does **Source A** explain the impact of the "Rough Wooing" on Scotland?   **6**

2. Describe the role of John Knox in the reformation in Scotland.   **4**

In **Source B** Mary Queen of Scots tried to communicate a message to Queen Elizabeth explaining her actions after the murder of Darnley.

Source B

> I am more upset than anyone at the tragic death of my husband: if my subjects had allowed me to act and if they had given me free use of my authority as Queen, I would have punished those responsible. I had no knowledge of who those people were and none of my subjects told me that those who are now held to be guilty of carrying out this crime were the ones most responsible for committing it; if they had done, I would certainly not have acted as I have up to now. I believe that I have done nothing except at the advice of the nobility of the realm.

3. Evaluate the usefulness of **Source B** as evidence of Mary Queen of Scots' actions at the time of the murder of Darnley.   **5**

   (You may want to comment on who wrote it, when they wrote it, why they wrote it, what they say or what has been missed out.)

4. Explain the reasons why Mary Queen of Scots was executed in 1587.   **6**

Sources **C** and **D** are about Mary Queen of Scots' involvement in the Ridolfi and Babington plots.

Source C

There is no doubt that Mary allowed herself to become embroiled in Babington's plot against Elizabeth, but this was entrapment pure and simple. Walsingham used double agents like Gifford to stir up Babington to write to Mary with his plan to overthrow Elizabeth and then added a deadly postscript to Mary's cautious reply to make absolutely sure of her guilt. For her part, Mary was driven by desperation after years of captivity to act recklessly. By contrast there is very little evidence to link Mary to the earlier plot hatched by the Italian banker Ridolfi.

Source D

Although she desperately backtracked once Ridolfi was unmasked, claiming she was the victim of forgery and exaggeration, it is implausible to believe that Mary was naïve enough to provide finance – which she admitted to – but not understand what was intended by the plotters. As for the Babington Plot, pleading entrapment, which was common practice in the 16th century and not illegal, could not hide that Mary was prepared to take any opportunity to depose her cousin as Queen of England.

5. Compare the views of **Sources C** and **D** about the role of Mary in the Ridolfi and Babington Plots. (Compare the sources overall and/or in detail.)   4

Part 4 – Migration and Empire, 1830–1939

Answer the following **five** questions using recalled knowledge and information from the sources where appropriate.

Sources A and **B** are about the reasons for Italian immigration to Scotland.

Source A

The primary reason for migration from Italy was poverty. Methods of land distribution and poor farming methods left many landless or trying to make a living from smaller and smaller plots of land. The secondary reason was overpopulation from the middle of the 19th century, leaving too many chasing too few jobs. From 1860 9 million left Southern Italy: Northern Italy, Northern Europe, America, Africa, Asia, England, Scotland, anywhere to escape the grinding poverty of the south.

Source B

Industrialisation and the jobs, prosperity and consumer goods that went with it came slowly to Italy and then mainly to the North. It was dreams of the $5 a day wealth in the factories of Detroit, the stories of unrivalled opportunities in New York, Chicago or the great cities of Northern Europe from relations that had gone before that drew Southern Italians in their millions – to America most of all. Some stopped off in Britain's cities on the way to get passage across the Atlantic and never left. Others, arriving in London or Manchester looked for new opportunities further afield and established businesses and livelihoods in prosperous industrialised towns and cities, in Glasgow, Edinburgh, Paisley, or Dundee.

1. Compare the views of **Sources C** and **D** about the reasons for Italian immigration to Scotland. (Compare the sources overall and/or in detail.)   **4**

2. Explain the reasons why people from Ireland and Europe arrived in Scotland in the 19th century.   **6**

Source C is about migration from the Highlands and Lowlands of Scotland in the 19th century.

Source C

There was undoubtedly coercion (use of force), with the many in arrears over their rent being offered a choice of a free passage or eviction from their crofts. Between 1841 and 1861 the population of the West Coast above Ardnamurchan and the Inner and Outer Hebrides went down by a third. After that, though emigration continued apace, it was largely from the Lowlands, driven not by destitution (extreme poverty), but by the prospect of better opportunities.

3. How fully does **Source C** explain the reasons for migration from Scotland in the 19th century?   **6**

Source D is an account of Irish sugar-workers in Greenock, 1836, from a Report on the State of the Irish Poor in Great Britain, Parliamentary Papers.

Source D

> Mr Thomas Fairrie, sugar manufacturer, of Greenock [stated] 'If it was not for the Irish, we should be obliged to import Germans, as is done in London. The Scotch will not work in sugar-houses; the heat drives them away in the first fortnight. If it was not for the Irish, we should be forced to give up trade; and the same applies to every sugar-house in town. This is a well-known fact. Germans would be our only resource, and we could not readily get them. Highlanders would not do the work'.

4. Evaluate the usefulness of **Source D** as evidence of the reaction to Irish immigrants in Scotland.   **5**

   (You may want to comment on who wrote it, when they wrote it, why they wrote it, what they say or what has been missed out.)

5. Describe the role played by Scots in the development of the British Empire between 1830 and 1939.   **4**

SECTION 2 – BRITISH CONTEXTS – 26 Marks

Attempt ONE part

Part 3 – War of the Three Kingdoms, 1603–1651

Answer the following **four** questions using recalled knowledge and information from the sources where appropriate.

Source A is from a speech given by King James VI/I to Parliament, March 1610.

Source A

> The state of monarchy is the supreme thing upon earth; for kings are not only God's lieutenants on earth and sit upon God's throne, but even by God himself are called gods. There are three things that illustrate the nature of monarchy: one from the Bible, the others from policy and philosophy. In the Scriptures kings are called gods and so their power can be compared to the divine power. Kings are also compared to the fathers of families, for the king truly is father of his country, the political father of his people. And lastly, kings are compared to the head of this microcosm (small model) of the body of man.

1. Evaluate the usefulness of **Source A** as evidence of the nature of Royal Authority 1603–25.   **5**

   (You may want to comment on who wrote it, when they wrote it, why they wrote it, what they say or what has been missed out.)

Source B is about Charles I's relations with Parliament during the 1620s.

Source B

> The strained relations between the King and Parliament in the early years of his reign are often attributed to religion. However, the true cause of the sequence of events that led to the Petition of Right and the imposition of the long period of personal rule fundamentally lay in finance. Parliament was not prepared to give the Crown sufficient funds to prosecute the war against Catholic Spain that they wanted him to pursue, but on the cheap. Charles was offended that they wanted to make him, God's anointed monarch, accountable for how he provisioned his armies. Restrictions on the collection of Tonnage and Poundage taxes, objections to his use of forced loans, went to the heart of Charles's idea of what good government was.

2. How fully does **Source B** explain why relations between King Charles and Parliament were so strained in the 1620s? (Use **Source B** and recall.)   **6**

3. To what extent did challenges to Royal Authority in Scotland cause the outbreak of war between Charles I and English Parliamentarians in 1641?   **9**

4. Explain the reasons why King Charles I was executed in 1649.   **6**

Part 4 – Changing Britain, 1760–1900

Answer the following **four** questions using recalled knowledge and information from the sources where appropriate.

1. Explain the reasons for housing problems in British cities in the first half of the 19th century. **6**

Source A is from an article in the *Scottish Railway Gazette* for April 1845.

Source A

> Railways will mean that all parts of the country will become more opened up. Land in the interior will, by a system of cheap and rapid transport for manure and farm produce, become almost as valuable as land on the coast. The man of business can as easily join his family at a distance of 10 or 12 miles as could formerly be done at 2 or 3 miles.

2. Evaluate the usefulness of **Source A** as evidence of the impact of railways on Britain. **5**

   (You may want to comment on who wrote it, when they wrote it, why they wrote it, what they say or what has been missed out.)

Source B is about the impact of legislation on working conditions in Britain in the 19th century.

Source B

> Robert Owen's significant efforts to have the conditions under which children worked in cotton factories addressed by Parliament culminated in the triumph of the Cotton Mills and Factories Act of 1819. Although the main focus of this Act was the employment of children, specifically those under nine, in cotton factories, the symbolic importance of this over time had an impact on safety, on hours and every other corner of working life in factories. Although it took time, the idea that the humane treatment of Britain's workers should be the concern of government was established.

3. How fully does **Source B** explain why the conditions of workers in Britain improved in the 19th century? (Use **Source B** and recall.) **6**

4. To what extent was Parliamentary Reform in the 19th century brought about by the actions of radical protesters? **9**

SECTION 3 – European and World – 29 Marks

Attempt ONE part

Part 5 – Red Flag: Lenin and the Russian Revolution, 1894–1921

Answer the following **five** questions using recalled knowledge and information from the sources where appropriate.

1. Describe the problems facing Russian agriculture and industry before 1905.   **4**

Sources A and **B** describe the Tsar's government of Russia between 1905 and 1914.

Source A

> The Tsar felt forced to promise a kind of constitution in October 1905. The Duma was very weak: it could not make laws, the Council of Ministers was selected by the Tsar and elections to the Duma were rigged to ensure that the nobility had the strongest representation and the more radical liberals were excluded. Even so, the Tsar resented sharing his ancient autocratic powers with anybody else. Having stepped away from the old ways of ruling, he tried to avoid having to deal with the Duma, cutting back its powers even more when he had the chance.

Source B

> The half-hearted concessions that the Tsar made in 1905 to share power with society represented by political parties neither made the regime more popular with the opposition nor raised his prestige with the people at large. They could not understand how a proper ruler could allow himself to be openly criticised by another government institution. His divine right to rule depended on his ability to rule forcefully. Nicholas II fell not because he was hated, but because he was held in contempt.

2. Compare the views of **Sources A** and **B** about the Tsar's government of Russia between 1905 and 1914. (Compare the sources overall and/or in detail.)   **4**

3. To what extent was the revolution of February 1917 caused by the government's mishandling of the Russian war effort?   **9**

Source C is about Order No. 1 issued on 1 March 1917.

Source C

> The Petrograd Soviet effectively controlled transport and communications and workers and soldiers looked to it for leadership. There was therefore 'dual power' because, while the Soviet was happy for the Provisional Government of the Duma to take control of the government, the Soviet itself had many of the reins of power. On 1 March it issued Army Order No 1: no one should do what the Provisional Government said unless the Soviet agreed.

4. How fully does **Source C** explain the failure of the Provisional Government in 1917? (Use **Source C** and recall.)   **6**

5. Explain the reasons why the Bolsheviks defeated the White forces in the Civil War.   **6**

Part 8 – Appeasement and the Road to War, 1918–1939

Answer the following **five** questions using recalled knowledge and information from the sources where appropriate.

Source A is about the Treaty of Versailles, signed in June 1918.

Source A

Germany was given two choices: either to sign the Treaty or to be invaded by the Allies.

They signed the Treaty as in reality they had no choice. When the ceremony was over, Clemenceau went out into the gardens of Versailles and said, "it is a beautiful day".

The Treaty seemed to satisfy the "Big Three" as in their eyes it was a just peace as it kept Germany weak yet strong enough to stop the spread of communism; kept the French border with Germany safe from another German attack and created the organisation, the League of Nations, that would end warfare throughout the world.

However, it left a mood of anger throughout Germany as it was felt that as a nation Germany had been unfairly treated.

1. How fully does **Source A** explain the consequences of the Treaty of Versailles? (Use **Source A** and recall.)   **6**

2. To what extent were the failures of the League of Nations due to its association with the Treaty of Versailles?   **9**

3. Explain the reasons why the Nazis adopted an aggressive foreign policy in the 1930s.   **6**

Sources B and **C** are about the reasons why Britain adopted a policy of Appeasement towards Germany in the 1930s.

Source B

The Government was concerned with the weakness of its armed forces, notably the lack of home defences, especially against the bomber. There had been widespread disarmament in the 1920s; there were no troops immediately available to mount a challenge.

The heads of Britain's armed forces – Chiefs of Staff – consistently warned Chamberlain that Britain was too weak to fight. Alongside this Nazi propaganda encouraged Britain and France to believe that Germany's forces were a lot stronger than they really were.

Source C

Appeasement was a reasonable response to the problems facing Britain in the 1930s. The British Empire stretched around almost a quarter of the globe and despite the strains of defending such an extensive area, dominion governments expressed limited enthusiasm for helping the mother country if drawn into a major conflict in Europe. The cost of defending an overseas empire with a strong navy conflicted with the demands of defending Britain from aerial threats and the possibility of a land war in Europe. Meanwhile there remained a strong pacifist mood in British society that politicians could not ignore.

4. Compare the views of **Sources B** and **C** about the reasons for the British policy of Appeasement. (Compare the sources overall and/or in detail.)   **4**

5. Describe the attempts to address German demands over Czechoslovakia in 1938.   **4**